NEON

This book is part of the Neon Library and was personally selected and introduced by:

JEFF CONSOLINO

The unique spirit of our people is what sets us apart and makes Neon glow.

These books are a lasting, evolving sample of both our culture and the vibrant relationships that Neon holds across the globe.

Please feel free to enjoy these pages, but leave them as you found them in the Neon Library.

CINCINNATI

OHIO

A PHOTOGRAPHIC PORTRAIT

Photography by J. Miles Wolf

Narrative by Linda Vaccariello

TWIN LIGHTS PUBLISHERS | ROCKPORT, MASSACHUSETTS

Copyright © 2017 by
Twin Lights Publishers, Inc.

All rights reserved. No part of this book may be reproduced in any form without written permission of the copyright owners. All images in this book have been reproduced with the knowledge and prior consent of the artists concerned and no responsibility is accepted by producer, publisher, or printer for any infringement of copyright or otherwise, arising from the contents of this publication. Every effort has been made to ensure that credits accurately comply with information supplied.

First published in the
United States of America by:

Twin Lights Publishers, Inc.
Rockport, Massachusetts 01966
Telephone: (978) 546-7398
www.twinlightspub.com

ISBN: 978-1-934907-52-8

10 9 8 7 6 5 4 3 2 1

(opposite)
Purple People Bridge

(frontispiece)
Cincinnati Skyline

(jacket front)
Roebling Bridge

(jacket back)
Roebling Bridge and Smale Riverfront Park

All photographs © 2017 by J. Miles Wolf

Book design by:
SYP Design & Production, Inc.
www.sypdesign.com

Printed in China

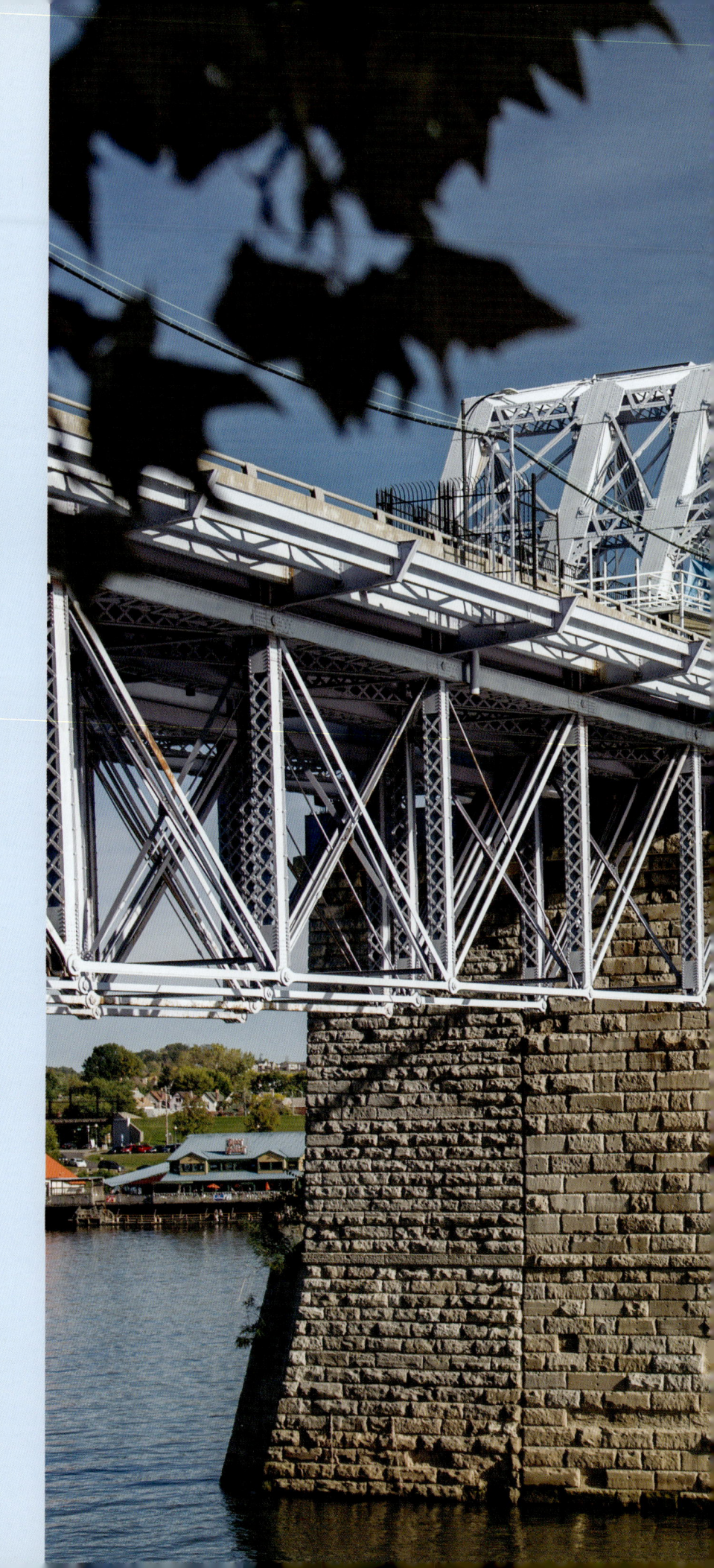

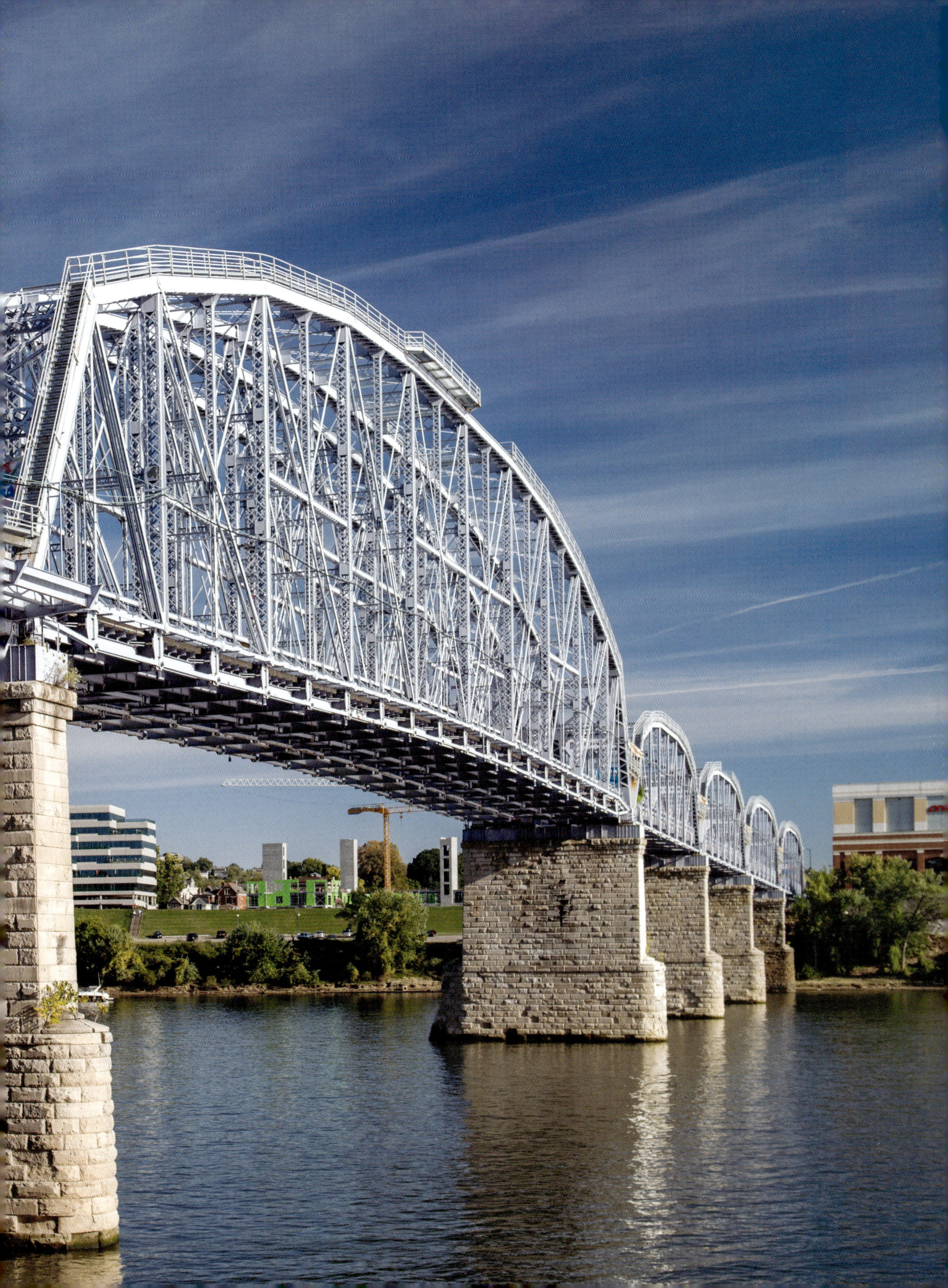

Sing the City Sculpture

The freestanding aluminum artwork is a testament to Cincinnatian's creativity, as well as their devotion. Asked to convey their feelings for their city in a word or phrase, citizens submitted 1,000 expressions of love. This sculpture is just one of 54 public art installations inspired by the 2015 project.

Where would you go to "see" Cincinnati? Is it possible to take in the essence of the town all at once?

Some people would tell you to drive across the river at dusk, turn around, and be enchanted as the city lights turn Cincinnati's skyline into a jeweled necklace. Others would send you to a single hilltop—maybe Eden Park, Mt. Echo, or Mt. Storm. Then you'd understand how Mother Nature shaped this place: green hillsides that frame the city; inclines so steep that no builder has tackled them; natural features that form subtle boundaries in this neighborhood-proud community.

A sports fan would recommend heading to the riverfront early on game day. Maybe take the kids for a ride on Carol Ann's Carousel at Smale Riverfront Park or grab a burger at The Banks, then, before you head into the game (Great American Ball Park when the Cincinnati Reds are in town, Paul Brown Stadium during the Bengals' season) drink in a long, long look at the Ohio River, the city's priceless liquid asset.

An architect might tell you to walk the streets to get a picture of what Cincinnati is all about. In a matter of blocks you can see an Art Deco masterpiece from the 1920s; a stunning center for 21st-century art; and street after street of narrow brick homes looking much as they did when German immigrants arrived before the Civil War, bringing their skills, their industrious discipline, and their love of faith and family.

But a young civic leader would probably tell you to simply take the Cincinnati Bell Connector—the city's new streetcar. It's the best way to see what's happening in Cincinnati today: a revitalized riverfront; a bustling downtown; public spaces alive with concerts, special events, and family gatherings; and historic neighborhood streets reborn block by block.

Everyone who lives in Cincinnati has a favorite way of regarding it—a scene or view or iconic moment that embodies this place we call home. From riverboats to bridges to the skyline's high-rise towers, J. Miles Wolf has captured the Queen City in *Cincinnati, Ohio: A Photographic Portrait*. Enjoy Cincinnati as he sees it. Perhaps your favorite view is here, too.

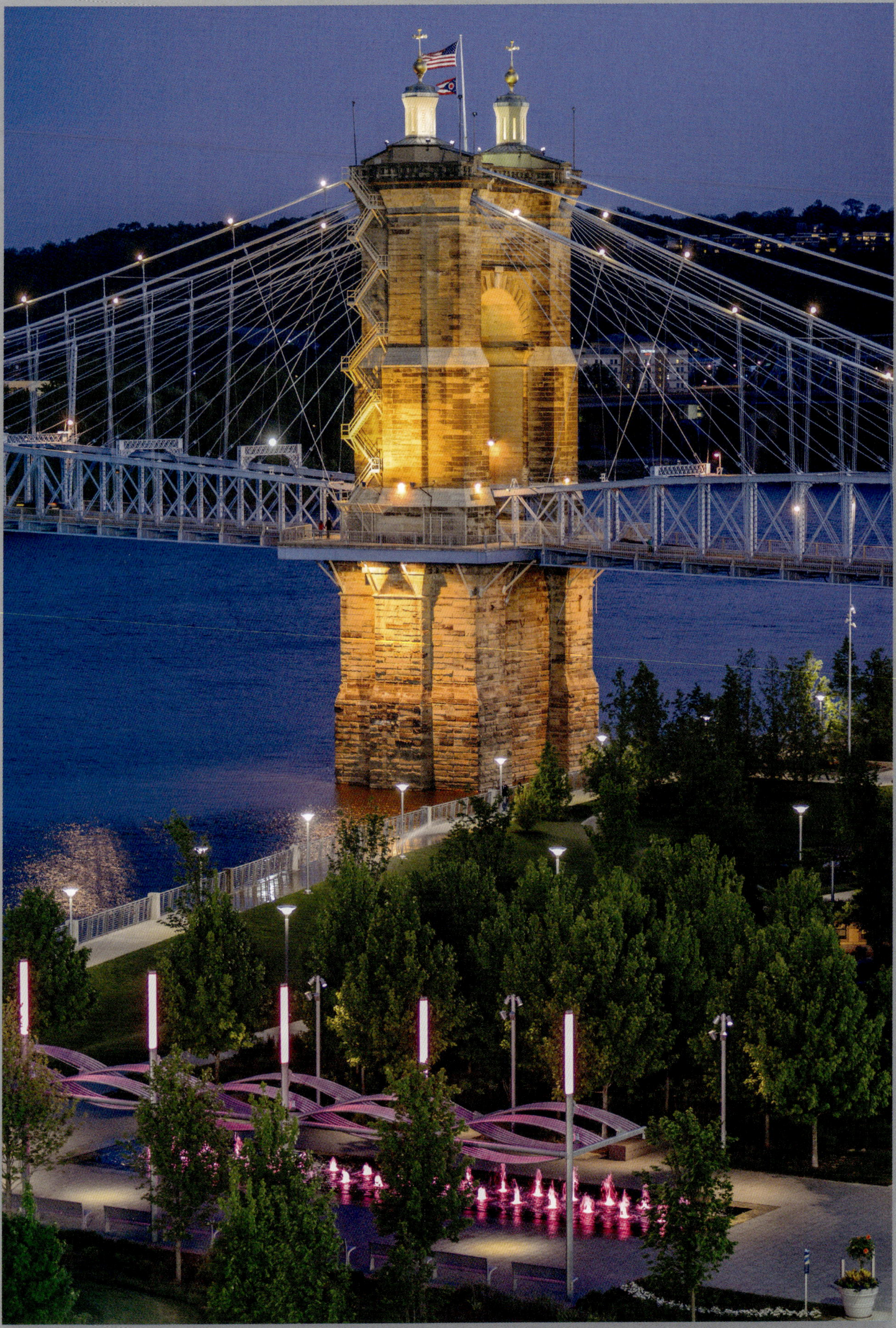

Roebling Bridge (opposite)

The 150-year-old John A. Roebling Suspension Bridge between Cincinnati and Covington, Kentucky, was begun before the Civil War, but wartime shortages delayed its completion until 1866. After it opened, Roebling, a civil engineer, began work on what would be his final, and most famous, project—the Brooklyn Bridge.

Daniel Carter Beard Bridge (top)

A pair of "golden arches" give this span its nickname—the Big Mac Bridge. Built in the 1970s, it carries Interstate 471 traffic from Cincinnati to Newport, Kentucky. The bridge is named for Kentuckian Daniel Carter Beard—artist, outdoorsman, and one of the founders of the Boy Scouts of America.

Riverboat (bottom)

Only nostalgic tourists travel by paddlewheel today. But river commerce remains an important part of the local economy. In 2016 the 226-mile-long region designated as the Ports of Cincinnati and Northern Kentucky was ranked the busiest inland port district in the nation by the US Army Corps of Engineers.

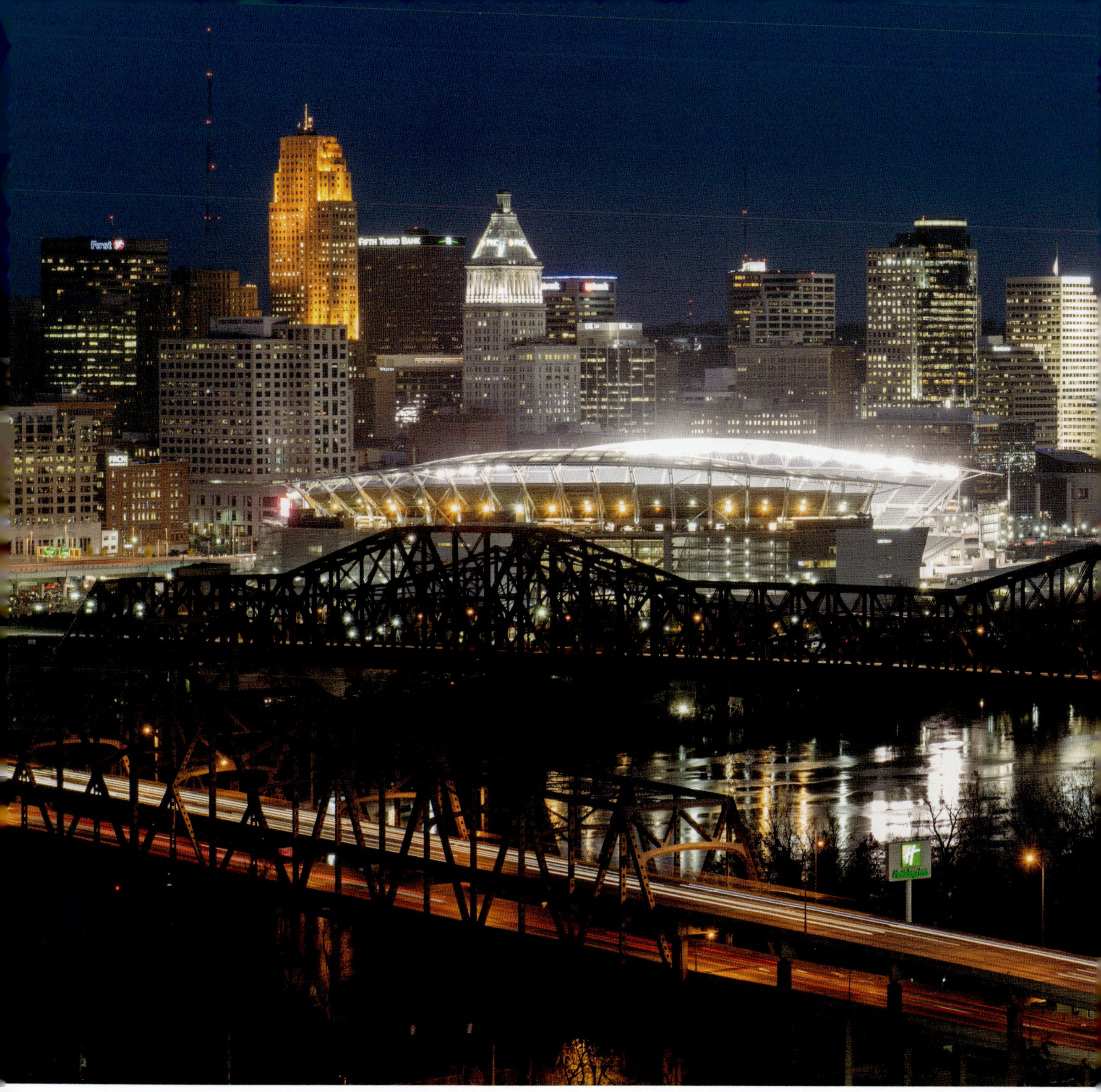
FIFTH THIRD BANK

Queen City

Henry Wadsworth Longfellow dubbed Cincinnati "The Queen of the West" in his 1854 poem, *Catawba Wine*, and ever since the town has been proud to be known as the Queen City. When the lights of downtown glow like jewels in a crown, the nickname seems perfect.

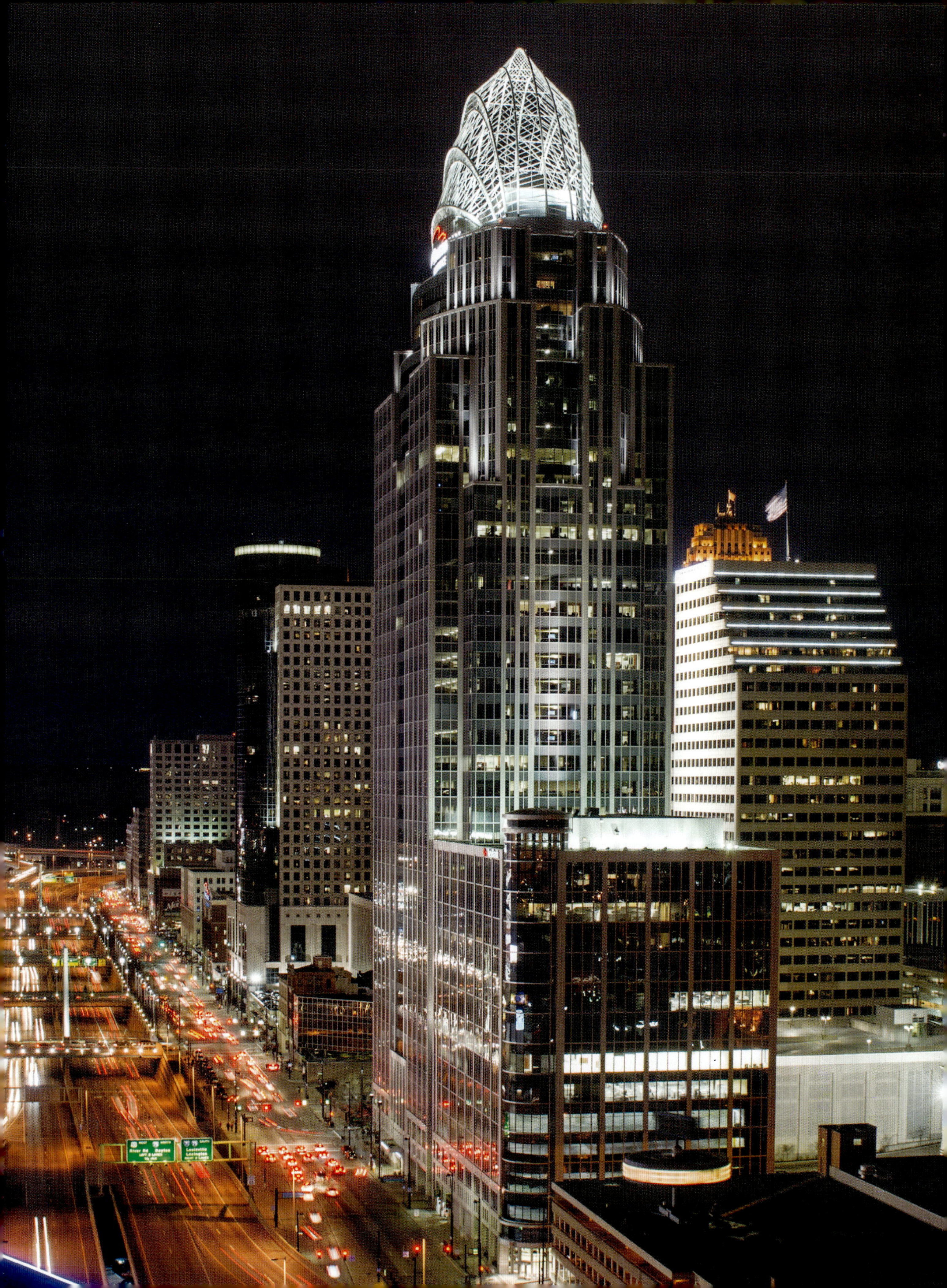

Great American Tower *(opposite)*

One of the most distinctive features in the skyline is the Great American Tower at Queen City Square. Completed in 2011, it's the city's tallest building. The firm of HOK designed it with a unique steel top inspired by a tiara worn by the late Princess Diana.

P&G Headquarters *(above)*

The multinational consumer goods giant Procter & Gamble makes its home here in a dramatic complex that spans two city blocks. P&G's postmodernist twin towers designed by the New York firm of Kohn Pedersen Fox greets travelers as they enter the city from the north on Interstate 71.

Carew Tower

Now on the National Register of Historic Places, the Carew Tower was begun in 1929 and completed in spite of the Great Depression. Rising 49 stories above Fountain Square on the southwest corner of 5th and Vine, the complex includes the Hilton Cincinnati Netherland Plaza hotel, an Art Deco masterpiece.

Tyler Davidson Fountain

For nearly 150 years—long before the sitcom *WKRP in Cincinnati* made it famous—the 43-foot-high brass and stone Tyler Davidson Fountain has been a beloved icon, and Fountain Square, where it sits, is a gathering place for the community. The graceful landmark is called The Genius of Water.

Tyler Davidson Fountain (above)

The fountain was gifted to the city from 19th-century merchant Henry Probasco in memory of his brother-in-law, Tyler Davidson. Rather than depicting mythic or heroic figures, the fountain's statues show ordinary people experiencing the blessing of water.

Tyler Davidson Fountain (opposite)

A spray of water washes over the bronze figure of a workman standing on a burning roof with an empty bucket, waiting for rain. The fountain, which was the work of the Royal Bronze Foundry of Bavaria, was dedicated in 1871.

Water Wall (pages 16–17)

Fountain Square, the plaza where the Genius of Water sits, was extensively remodeled in 2006. The broad, welcoming plaza now includes a granite wall where water spills over the final stanzas of *Catawba Wine*—the poem by Henry Wadsworth Longfellow that gave the Queen City its nickname.

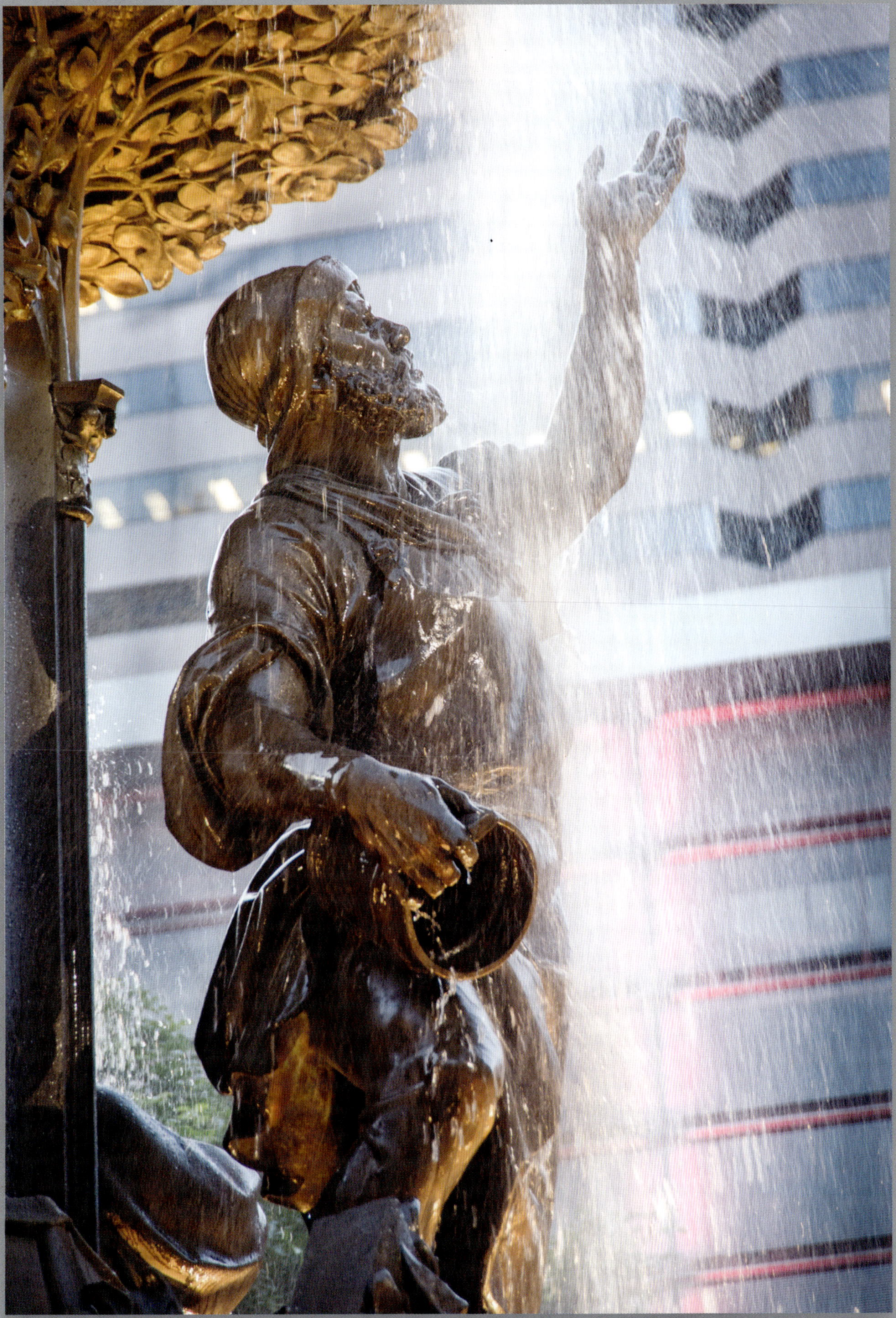

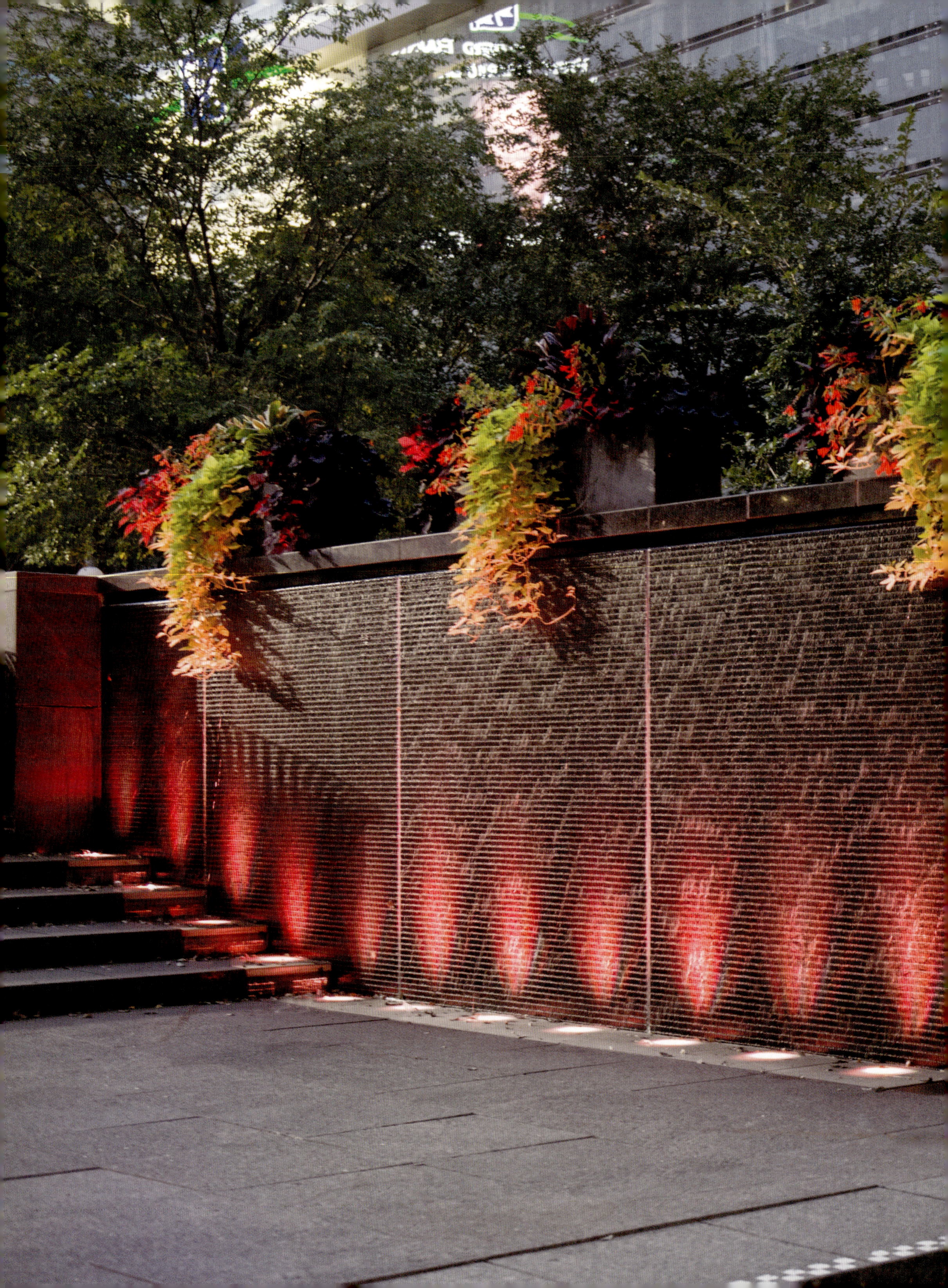

AND THIS SONG OF THE VINE,
THIS GREETING OF MINE,
THE WINDS AND THE BIRDS SHALL DELIVER
TO THE QUEEN OF THE WEST,
IN HER GARLANDS DRESSED,
ON THE BANKS OF THE BEAUTIFUL RIVER.

—HENRY WADSWORTH LONGFELLOW

Times-Star Building (above and left)

The dramatic Art Deco building at 800 Broadway was once home to *The Cincinnati Times-Star,* and later the *Cincinnati Post.* Carved figures on four corners of the tower represent Truth, Speed, Patriotism, and Progress—qualities of a good newspaper. Today it is used by Hamilton County.

PNC Center

This early 20th-century skyscraper is officially named the 4th and Vine Tower. When it was completed in 1913, it was the tallest building outside of Manhattan. Designed by Cass Gilbert (creator of New York's famed Woolworth Building), it features a distinctive top that looks like a Grecian temple.

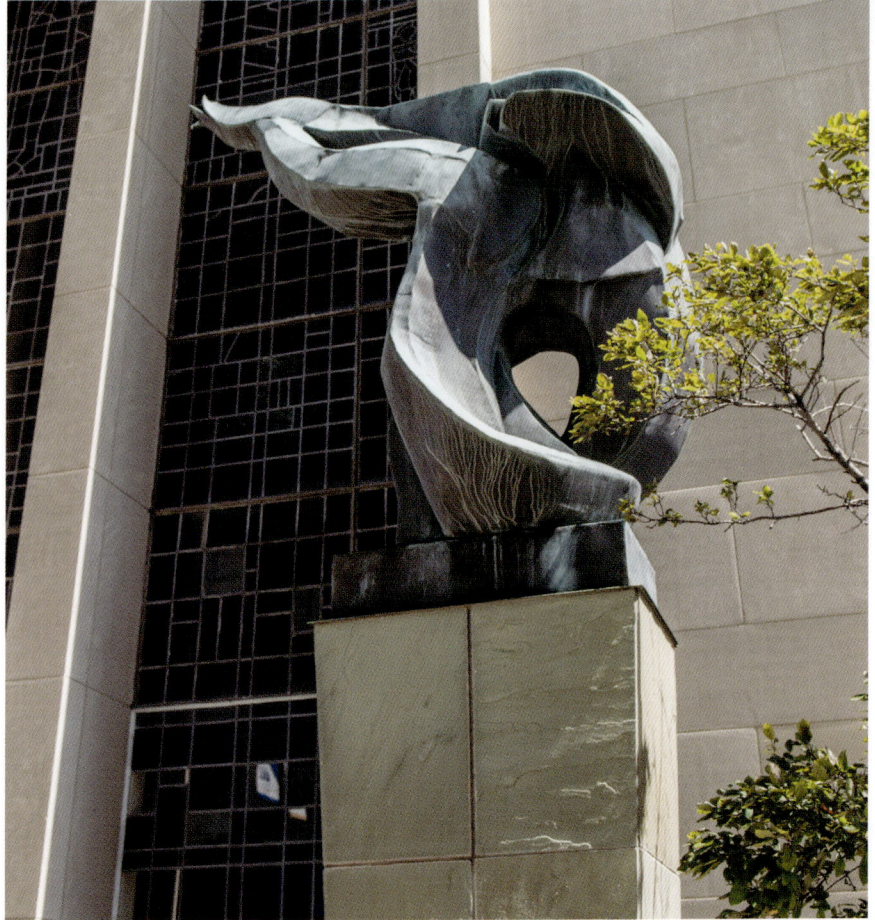

Carriage Rides *(above)*

Horse-drawn carriages queue up for riders at 5th and Vine, opposite Fountain Square, which bustles with winter activities during the holiday season. Fountain Place, on the west side of the square, includes a bookstore, Macy's department store, and jeweler Tiffany & Co.

Charles P. Taft Memorial *(left)*

Poised in front of Christ Church Cathedral at 318 E. Fourth Street, an abstract sculpture by artist Timothy Werrell commemorates Charles P. "Charlie" Taft. The son of President William Howard Taft served as mayor and councilman, and his devotion to his hometown earned him the name of "Mr. Cincinnati."

Venus Statue *(above)*

Internationally-renowned artist Jim Dine based his work *Cincinnati Venus* on the 2nd-century B.C. Greek masterpiece, *Venus de Milo*. In addition to being armless, Dine's version has no head. The verdigris bronze statue, a gift to the city in 1988, sits on Centennial Plaza at 895 Central Ave.

Library Fountain *(pages 22–23)*

Looking like a tumble of books on a giant's bed stand, the Amelia Valerio Weinberg Memorial Fountain greats visitors at the main branch of the Public Library of Cincinnati and Hamilton County. The library dates to 1853, making it the oldest public library west of the Alleghenies.

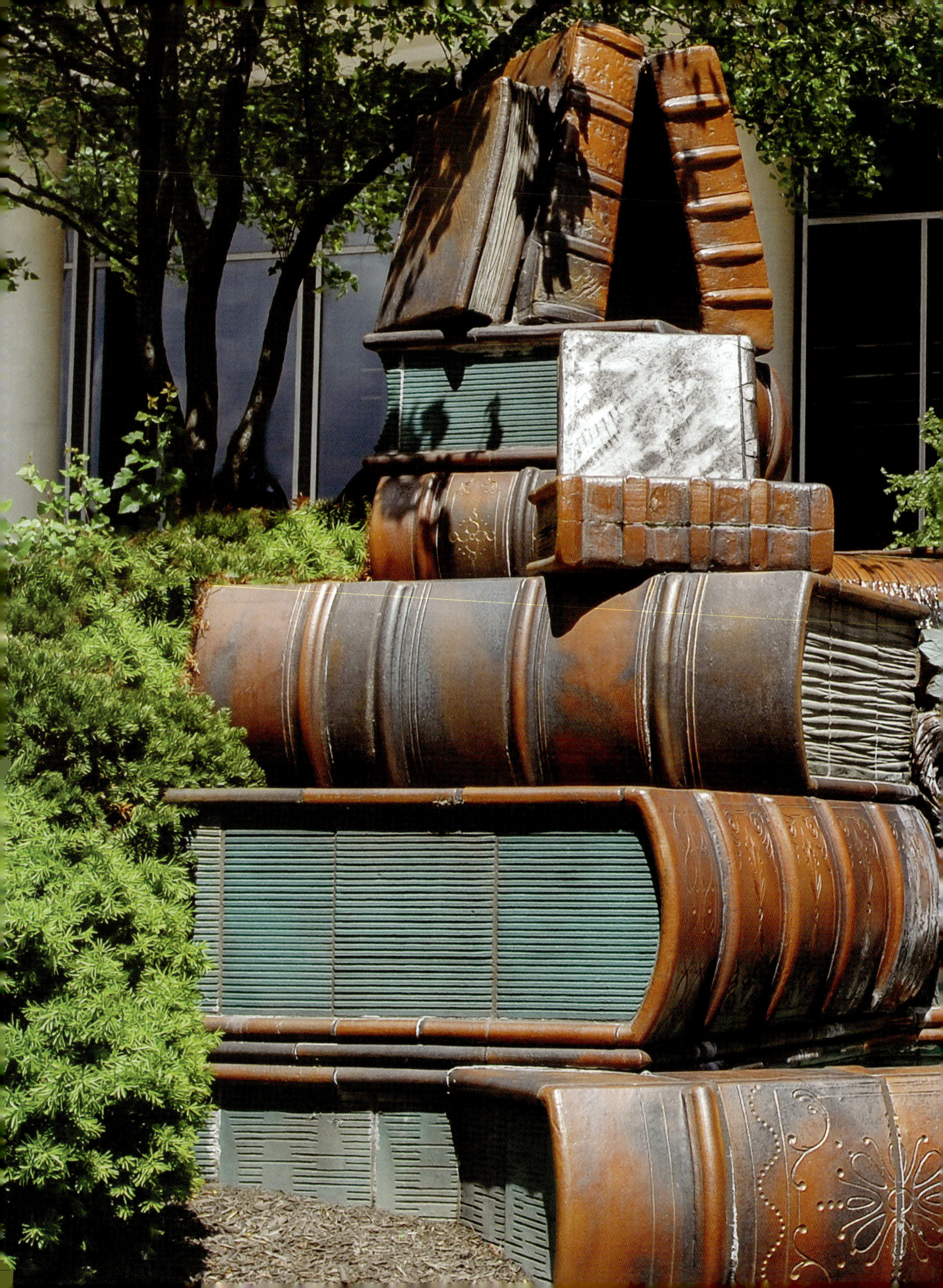

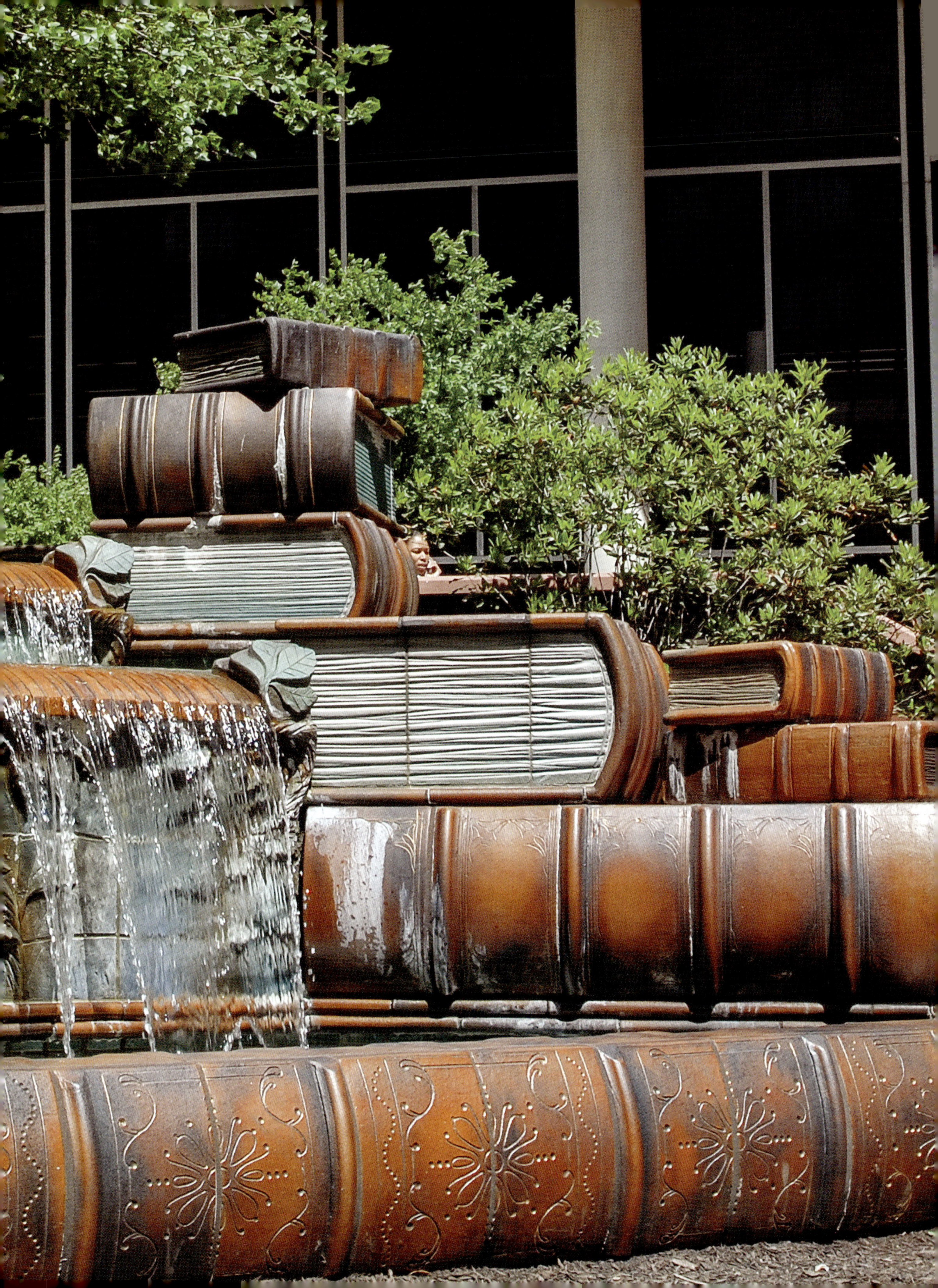

24

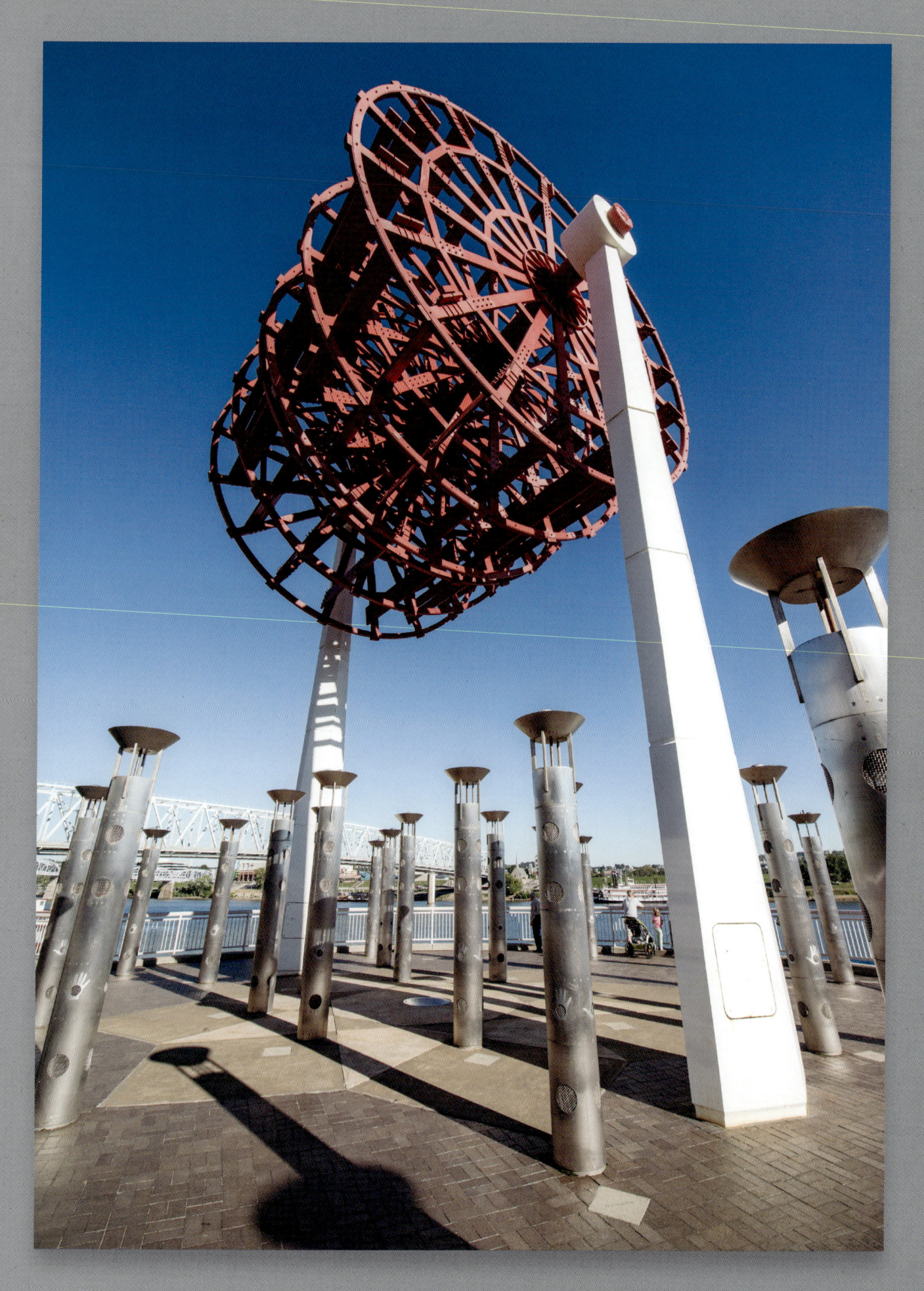

Daniel Carter Beard Bridge (above)

As the eastern-most river-crossing in downtown Cincinnati, the twin-span Daniel Carter Beard bridge carries heavy commuter traffic to and from Northern Kentucky. Bright yellow paint on the span's arches accounts for its more common name—"The Big Mac." McDonald's once considered building a floating restaurant nearby.

Cincinnati Bell Connector (right)

It's an old idea that's driving new development. The Cincinnati Bell Connector is a modern streetcar on a 3.6-mile loop that links residential, employment, and entertainment centers in downtown, the riverfront, and the city's rapidly transforming Over-the-Rhine neighborhood. Inaugurated in the fall of 2016, it runs every day, year-round.

National Steamboat Monument (opposite)

Before the Civil War, the Queen City bustled with steamboats carrying passengers and goods. Visitors to Public Landing can stand under the three-story, 60-ton replica of a riverboat paddle wheel surrounded by 24 metal "smokestacks" and contemplate an era when these giants churned along the river.

Roebling Bridge

Some 19th-century Cincinnatians didn't want the bridge: they feared losing business to Kentucky. So it was stipulated that it couldn't line up with any Cincinnati thoroughfare. Today the entrance on the Ohio side begins at a small traffic circle in The Banks—still slightly off-kilter from any city street.

Roebling Bridge (*above and pages 28–29*)

The bridge's fame increased during the Flood of 1937. Walls of sandbags held back the water at its Cincinnati and Covington entrances, making it the only Ohio River crossing for 800 miles during the disaster. Owned by the Commonwealth of Kentucky, it is designated a National Historic Landmark.

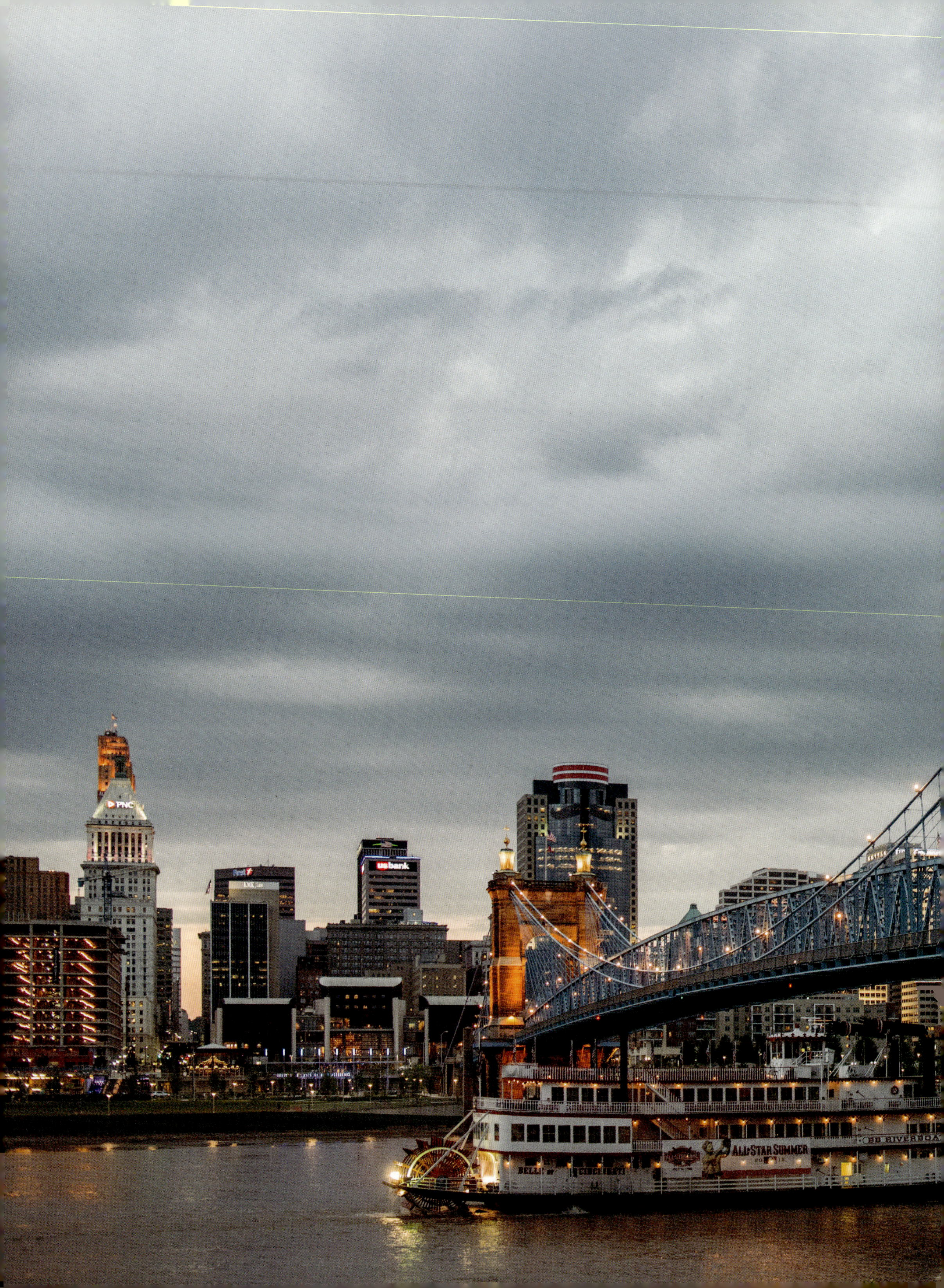
PNC
usbank
ALL STAR SUMMER

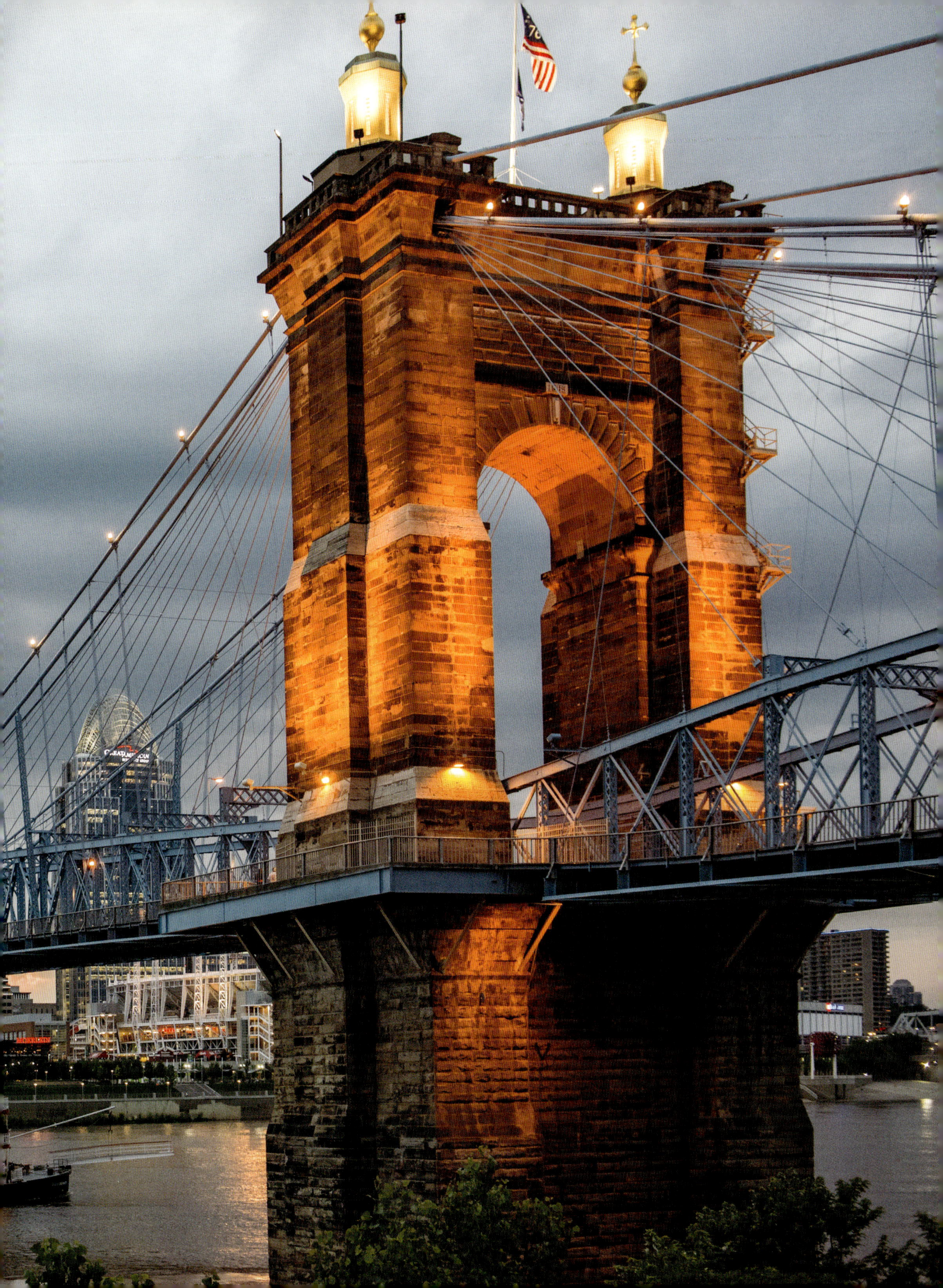

BROTHERS
BROTHERS
EST. 1967
BARNES & NOBLE
BOOKSELLERS
NEWPORT ON THE LEVEE
RIVERWALK

W
E

Riverwalk *(opposite bottom)*

Popular with joggers, strollers, and outdoor diners, Newport's Riverwalk is one leg of a planned 11-mile recreational path that will ultimately serve six communities on the south bank of the Ohio River. With great city views, the project is the work of Southbank Partners, a regional community and economic development organization.

Newport on the Levee
(opposite top and above)

Day and night, the walkway bustles with shoppers, tourists, and families on their way to Newport on the Levee's AMC multiplex cinema and the Newport Aquarium. Beyond the obvious economic and quality-of-life benefits, redevelopment has included river eco-system restoration and riverbank stabilization.

View from Devou

Once a family farm, today the 700+ acre Devou Park in Covington, Kentucky, includes picnic shelters, playing fields, hiking and mountain biking trails, a golf course, and this breathtaking overlook of Cincinnati. It's also home to the Behringer-Crawford Museum, which explores the unique archeology, history, and culture of Northern Kentucky.

Downtown Stadiums

You can't miss the swoosh of scarlet that belongs to the Cincinnati Reds' Great American Ball Park. In front of it is US Bank Arena, home of Cincinnati Cyclones Hockey. And beyond, the city's football mecca: Cincinnati Bengals' Paul Brown Stadium.

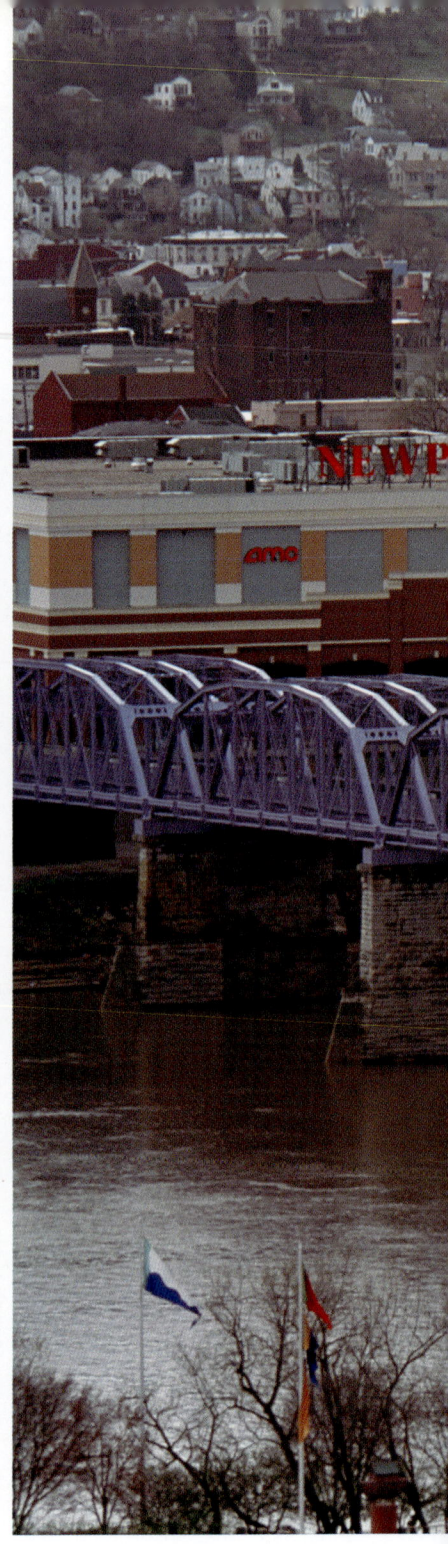

Purple People Bridge

(top, bottom, and opposite)

Officially it's the Newport Southbank Bridge, but once the disused auto and train bridge was restored, painted purple, and reopened for foot traffic, the cheekier name was a shoo-in. At 2,670 feet long, the Purple People Bridge is the longest pedestrian bridge in the country linking two states.

35

Riverboats (above)

The *Belle of Cincinnati* and the *River Queen* still ply the waters of the Ohio. Operated by Kentucky-based BB Riverboats, the vessels offer sightseeing outings, special event cruises, and private charters. Decorated in the ornate style of the past, they're a journey back to a simpler time.

South Bank (opposite)

Old and new combine along the river in Covington, Kentucky, showcasing the dynamic lines of The Ascent at Roebling's Bridge, a residential high rise designed by New York architect Daniel Libeskind. The swoop of the Covington building mimics the bridge's cables and gives every resident a breathtaking view of Cincinnati.

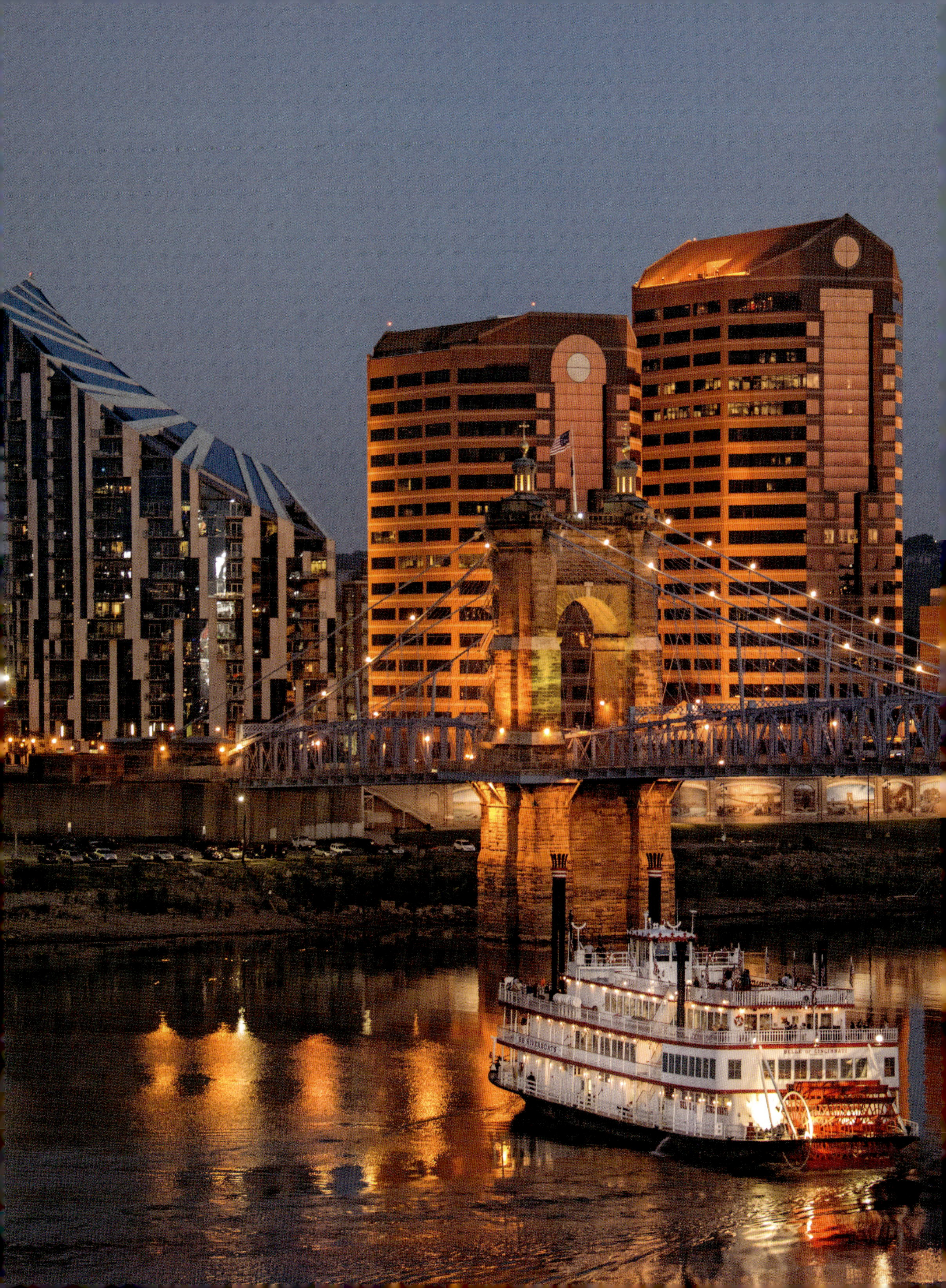

Ohio River *(top and bottom)*

What's the finest view in the city? Cincinnatians can't agree on the best direction, much less the best spot. Consider the vista from the Twin Lakes overlook in Eden Park. Whether you look east toward the river's lazy bend (top) or turn west toward downtown (bottom), sunsets are spectacular.

Barge Traffic

Coal moves slowly upstream on a quiet day on the river. The Ports of Cincinnati and Northern Kentucky move about 48 million tons of cargo a year—ranking 15th among all U.S. ports. Add in recreational boating and pleasure travel, and the beautiful Ohio River is a busy place.

Taft Historic Site

In 1857 the home at 2038 Auburn Avenue was the birthplace of the 27th president of the United States (and later Supreme Court Justice) William Howard Taft. Today, the elegant Greek Revival mansion is open to the public as a National Historic Site.

Taft Museum of Art

William Howard Taft's half-brother and sister-in-law, Charles Phelps Taft and his wife Anna, gave their house, ca 1820, at 316 Pike Street and their art collection to create a museum. The collection includes Chinese porcelains, French enamels, and paintings by artists as varied as Rembrandt, Gainsborough, and John Singer Sargent.

William Henry Harrison Statue

The war hero and 9th U.S. president is captured astride his horse in this monument created in 1896. William Henry Harrison lived in the settlement of North Bend between Cincinnati and the Indiana border. He was elected president only to die of pneumonia a month after his 1841 inauguration.

James Garfield Statue

To the east of the Harrison statue, in lovely tree-lined Piatt Park, is a monument to another Ohio son, President James A. Garfield. The park, which runs down the center of Eighth Street for two blocks, has been a green oasis downtown since the late 19th century.

44

Abraham Lincoln Statue (opposite)

Charles Phelps Taft and his wife Anna commissioned the statue that sits in the Lytle Park historic district—an 11-foot bronze by George Grey Barnard that captures a beardless, sober Lincoln seemingly weighed down with worries. Taft Museum faces the park at the east end of Fourth Street.

Hyde Park (above)

The Kilgour Fountain provides a gathering spot in the eastside neighborhood of Hyde Park. A community of large homes and broad streets, Hyde Park was developed at the turn of the 20th century and remains one of the city's most popular neighborhoods.

Ault Park *(above and left)*

Beautiful plantings and spectacular views of the river valley help make Ault Park one of the city's most-visited outdoor destinations. The magnificent Grand Pavilion has hosted scores of weddings and special events. One of these is the annual Concours d'Elegance, when owners of vintage automobiles gather to showcase their vehicles.

Spring in Ault Park

Cherry blossoms usher in spring on the park's rolling hills. The flowering trees were first planted here in 1932 by the Garden Club of Cincinnati to memorialize those who died in WWI. Summer brings another popular community event, the Independence Day fireworks celebration.

Probasco Fountain *(above)*

In 1887, horses would drink from the fountain's lower basin. Today it's a spot for relaxing in the pedestrian-friendly neighborhood of Clifton. The fountain was the gift of businessman Henry Probasco, who was also responsible for the Tyler Davidson Fountain in downtown Cincinnati.

Gateway Monument *(opposite)*

Drivers approaching downtown from the east are greeted by the abstract sculpture at 5th and Pike streets. The artwork is one of several which are part of the city's Gateway project, established 25 years ago to enliven the various points of entry to the city.

49

Eden Park

The nearly 200-acre park in the hills above downtown was once a vineyard. Nineteenth century millionaire Nicholas Longworth grew grapes here during the 1830s and 40s and dubbed the spot "The Garden of Eden." Blight ruined the local wine industry before the Civil War, but not the beauty of the location.

Eden Park

The park, which lies between the neighborhoods of Mt. Adams and Walnut Hills, is home to the Cincinnati Playhouse and the Cincinnati Art Museum. Picturesque features such as the ornate gazebo (opposite) and this 1894 water tower date to its earliest days.

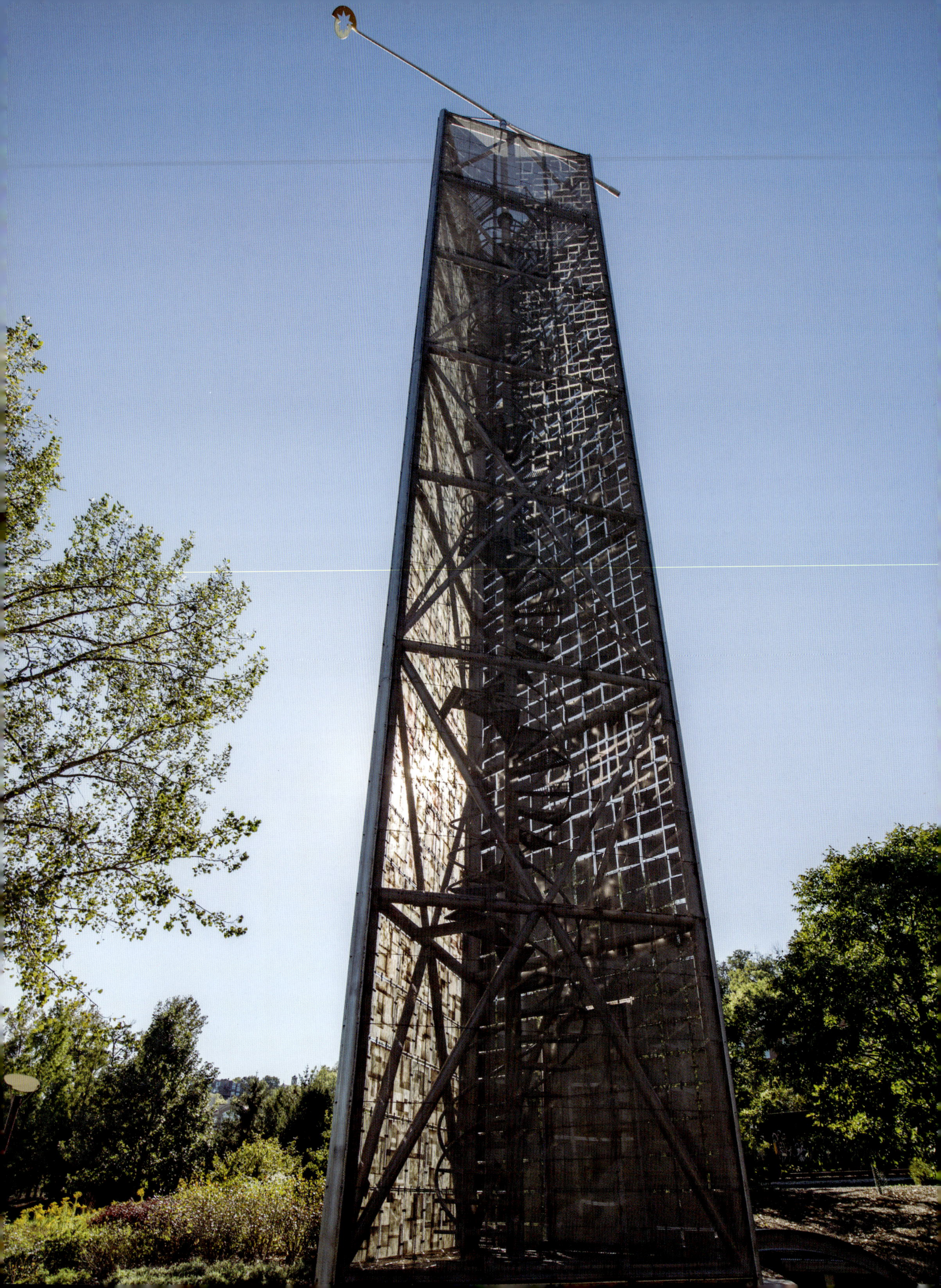

Crystalline Tower *(opposite)*

Made of titanium, mica, and steel mesh, the 90-foot tower in the Theodore M. Berry International Friendship Park glints in the sun. In keeping with the park's international theme, the work was a collaboration between Ohio artist Susan Ewing and Czech sculptor Vratislav Novak.

Seven Vessels Sculpture

(above and pages 54–55)

A contrast to the nearby metallic Crystalline Tower, Welsh sculptor David Nash's *Seven Vessels Ascending/Descending* gets its drama from pillars made of fire-singed oak. The work is oriented so that at midday on the summer solstice, sunlight shines through a long notch on one of the oaken vessels.

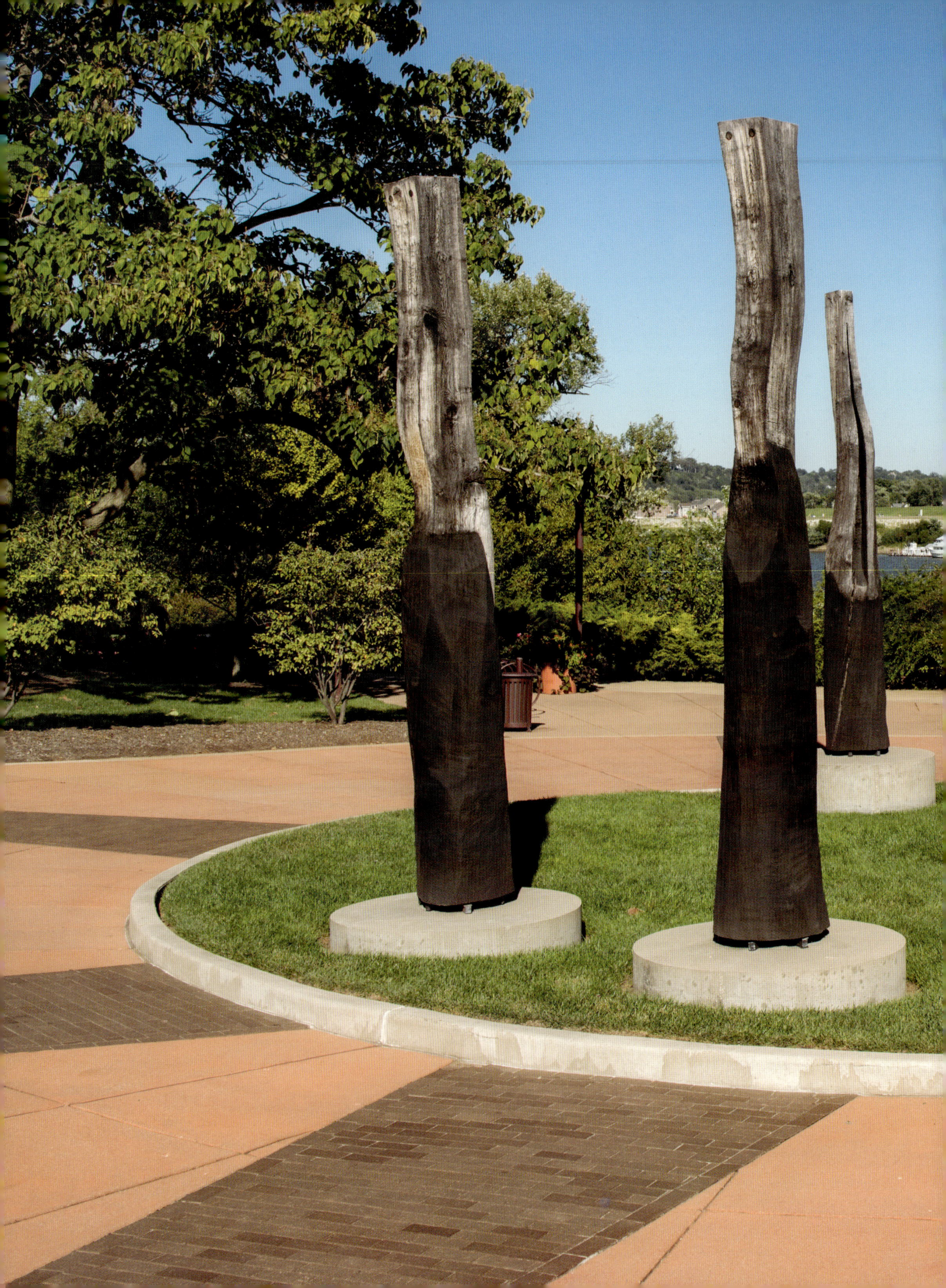

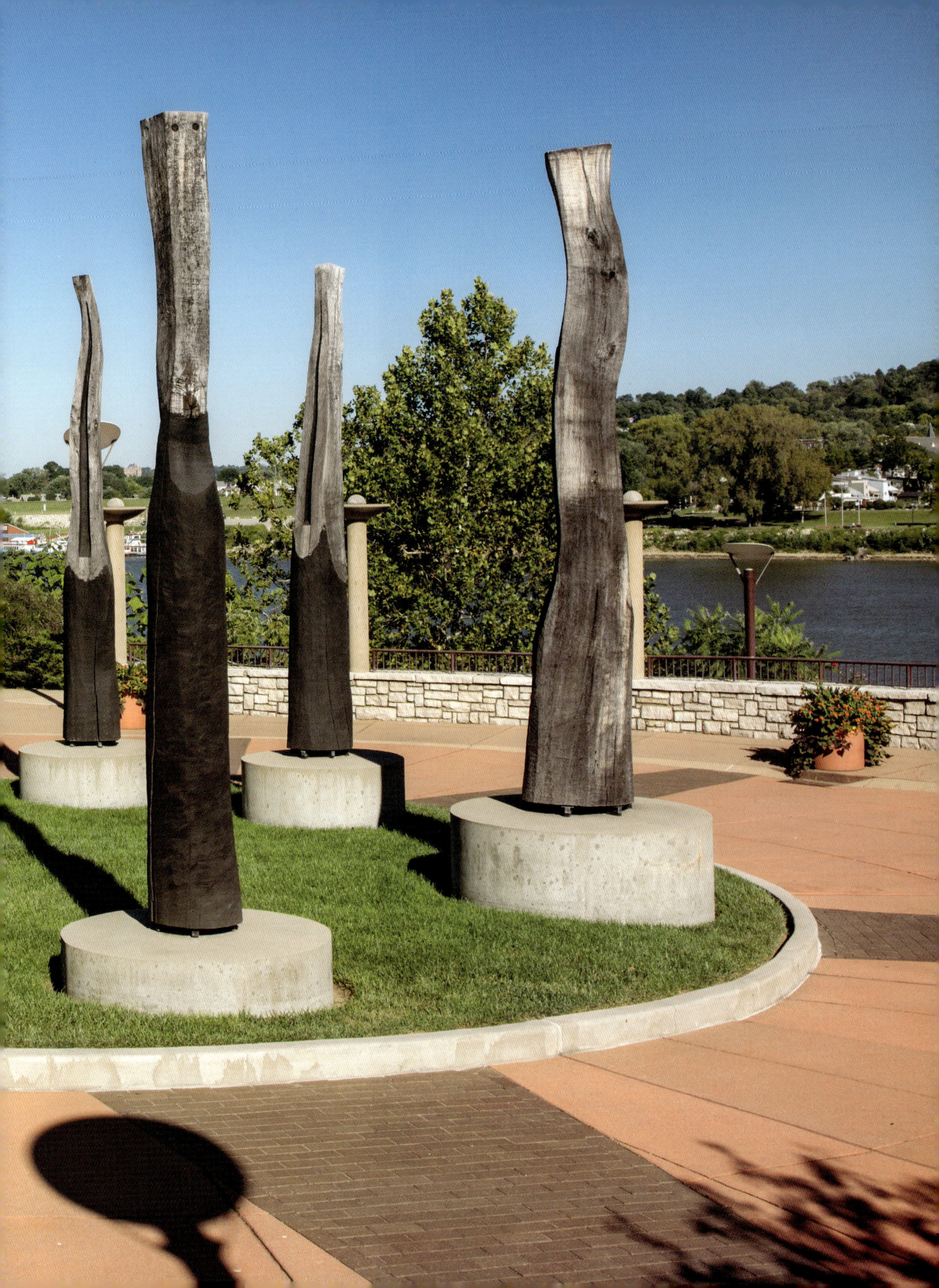

Friendship Park (above and left)

Global peace and unity is the theme behind the Theodore M. Berry International Friendship Park east of downtown. Named in honor of the city's first African-American mayor, it contains sculptures and plantings that represent five continents. The paths that hug the riverside intertwine like a child's friendship bracelet.

Friendship Park (opposite)

The park's sparkling *Castle of Air* mirrors the sky and scenery, making the structure itself seem to disappear. It was a 2004 gift from the city of Munich, Cincinnati's Sister City in Germany. Like other sculptures in the park, this was created by an international artist—Peter Haimerl of Munich.

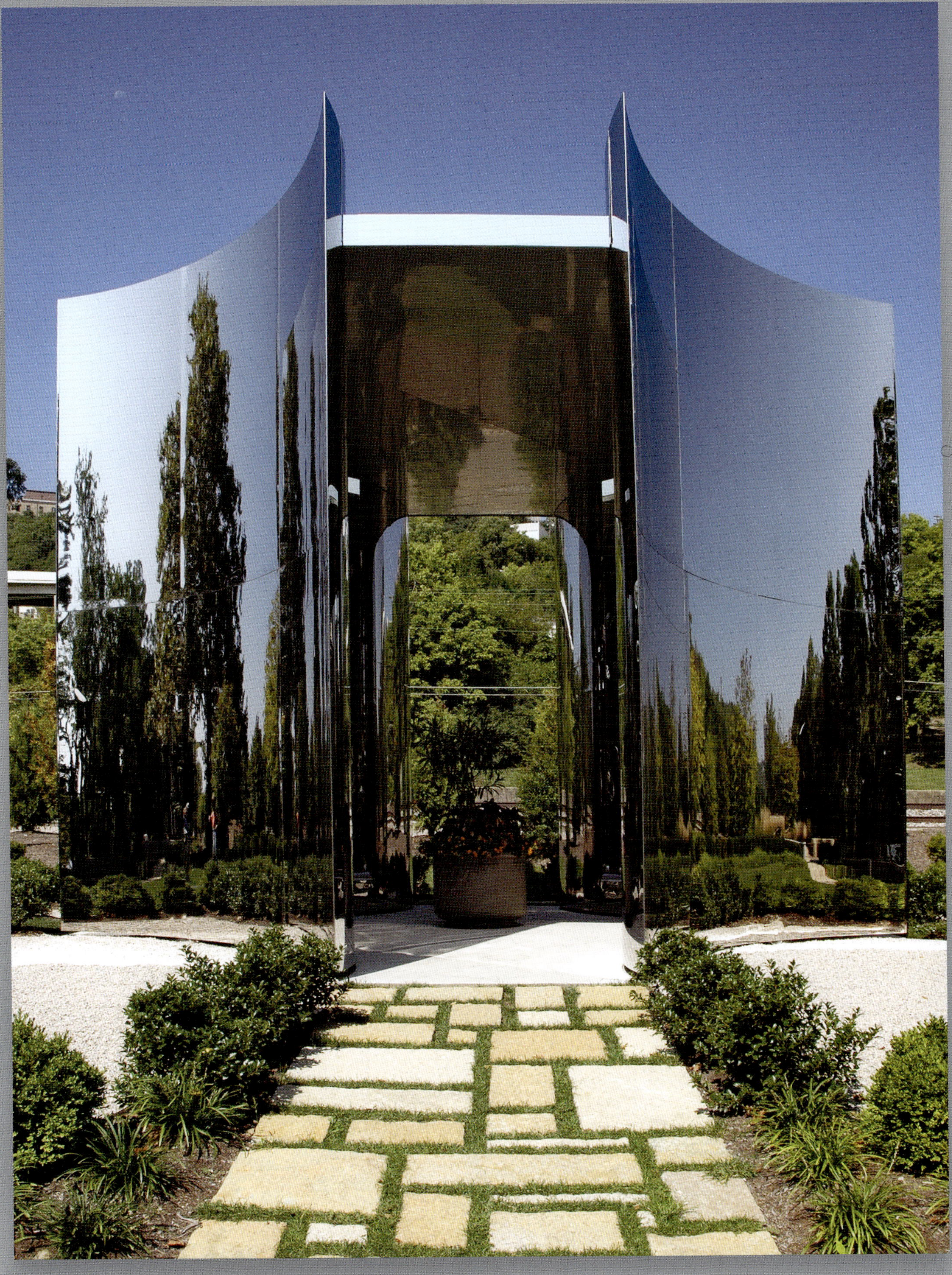

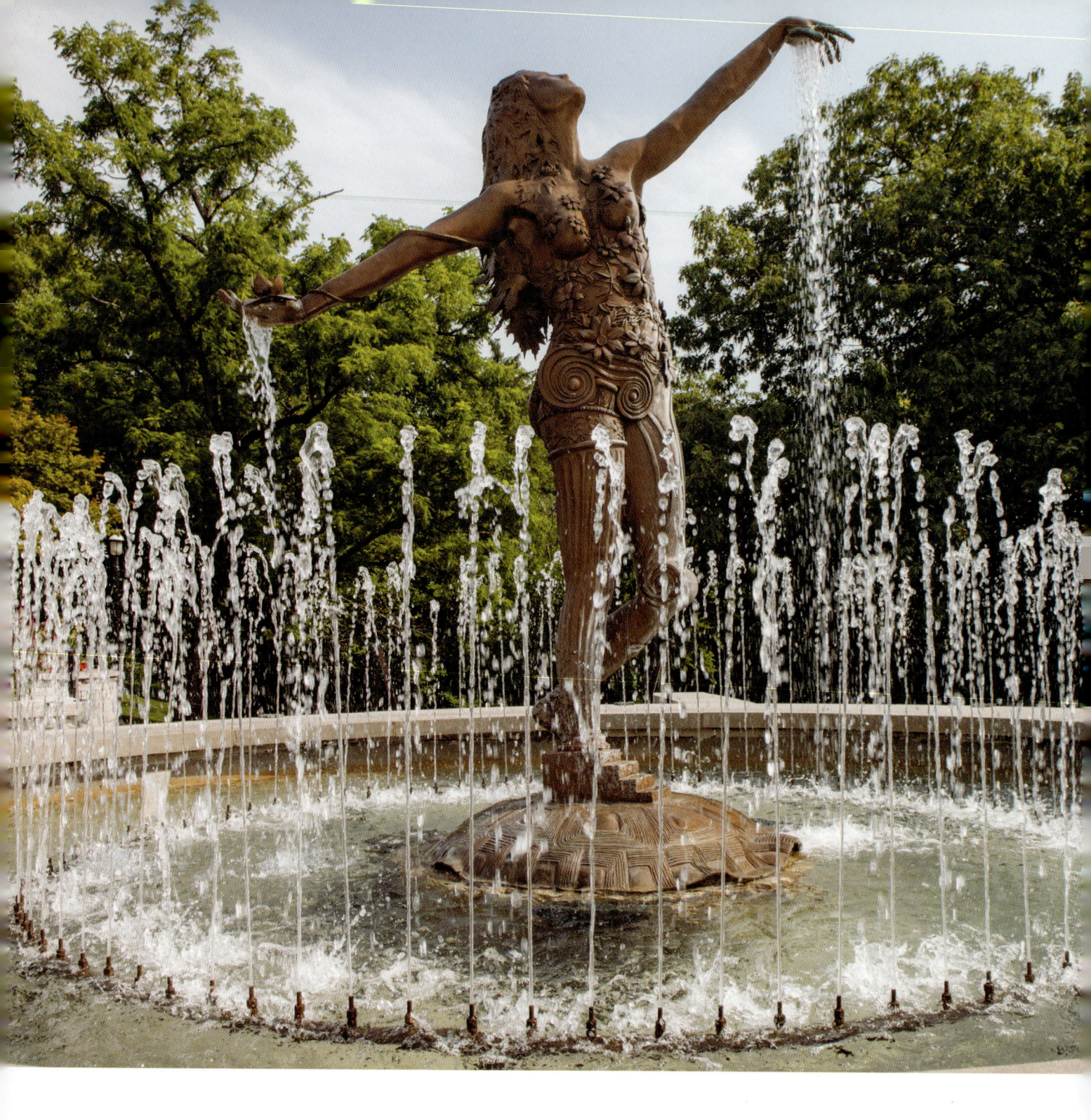

Woman Offering Water Sculpture

The cavorting flower child at the corner of Ludlow and Clifton avenues is a tribute to the creative spirit that prevails in the Clifton neighborhood, a place of shops, restaurants, and old fashioned gaslights. *Woman Offering Water* was designed by local artist Matt Kotlarczyk, an alumnus of the University of Cincinnati.

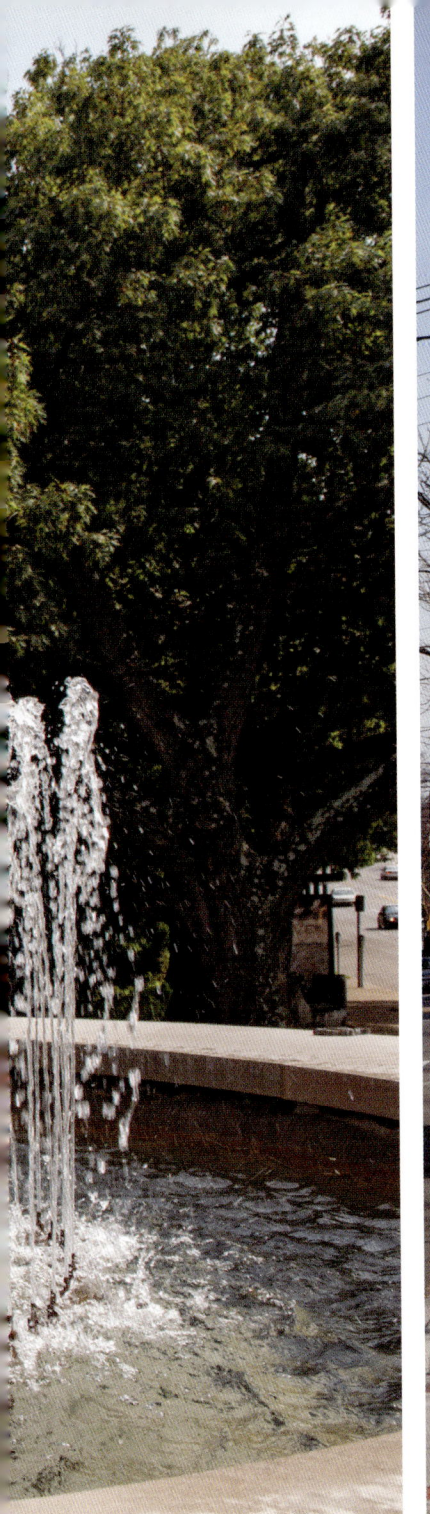

Clifton

Located not far from the sprawling University of Cincinnati campus and the hospitals of "pill hill," the Clifton neighborhood has a vibe that is both youthful and historic. The lively business district includes the community's original movie theater, now redeveloped to show art films and independent flicks.

Burnet Woods

In 1874, 90-acre Burnet Woods Park opened to the public, and has remained a popular spot ever since. The Trailside Nature Center facility was built by the Works Progress Administration. Today it is handicapped accessible and is used for nature programs.

Burnet Woods Bandstand

The Victorian bandstand in Burnet Woods Park continues to be a popular hangout for University of Cincinnati students. The park includes a man-made lake, hiking trails, picnic areas, and the tiny, low-tech Wolff Planetarium—the oldest planetarium outside of the East Coast.

Bishop's Place (above)

In the second half of the 19th century, a handful of wealthy businessmen were drawn to a sweeping hillside at the edge of Clifton known as Mt. Storm. The Chateauesque-style Bishop's Place at 429 Lafayette Avenue is one of the awe-inducing mansions built by these "barons of Mt. Storm."

Immaculata Church (opposite)

In good weather and foul, generations of Catholics have gathered at the foot of the hill below Holy Cross-Immaculata in Mt. Adams on Good Friday. The tradition is to ascend to the church, praying the rosary or some other devotional on each one of the 96 steps.

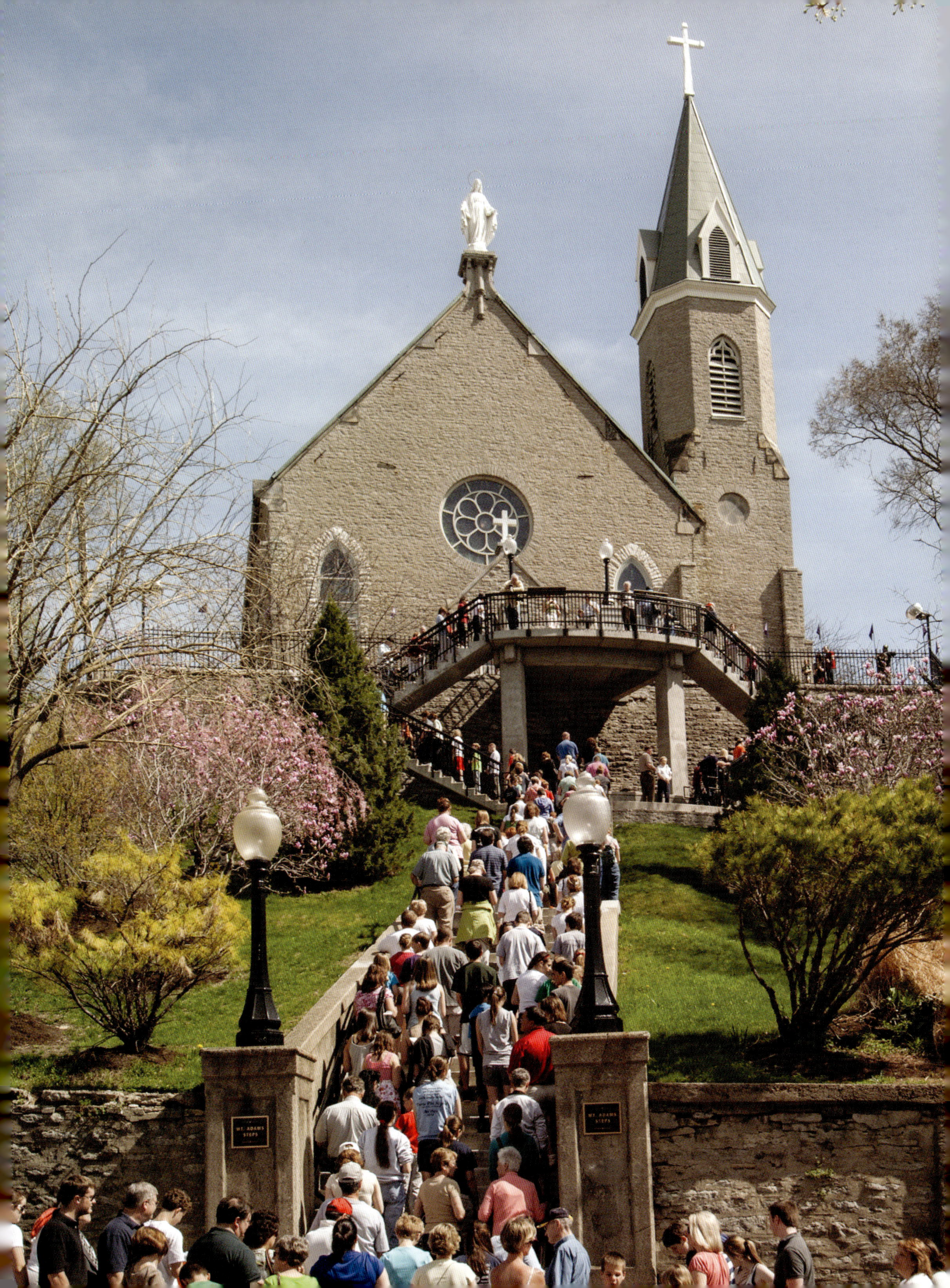
MT. ADAMS STEPS
MT. ADAMS STEPS

Isaac M. Wise Temple

(above and opposite)

Begun in the early 1860s and completed after the Civil War, it was here that Rabbi Isaac M. Wise explored his ideas for a religious movement that would come to be known as Reform Judaism. Inside and out, the complex architecture hints at a variety of influences—Gothic, Islamic, Byzantine, and Moorish.

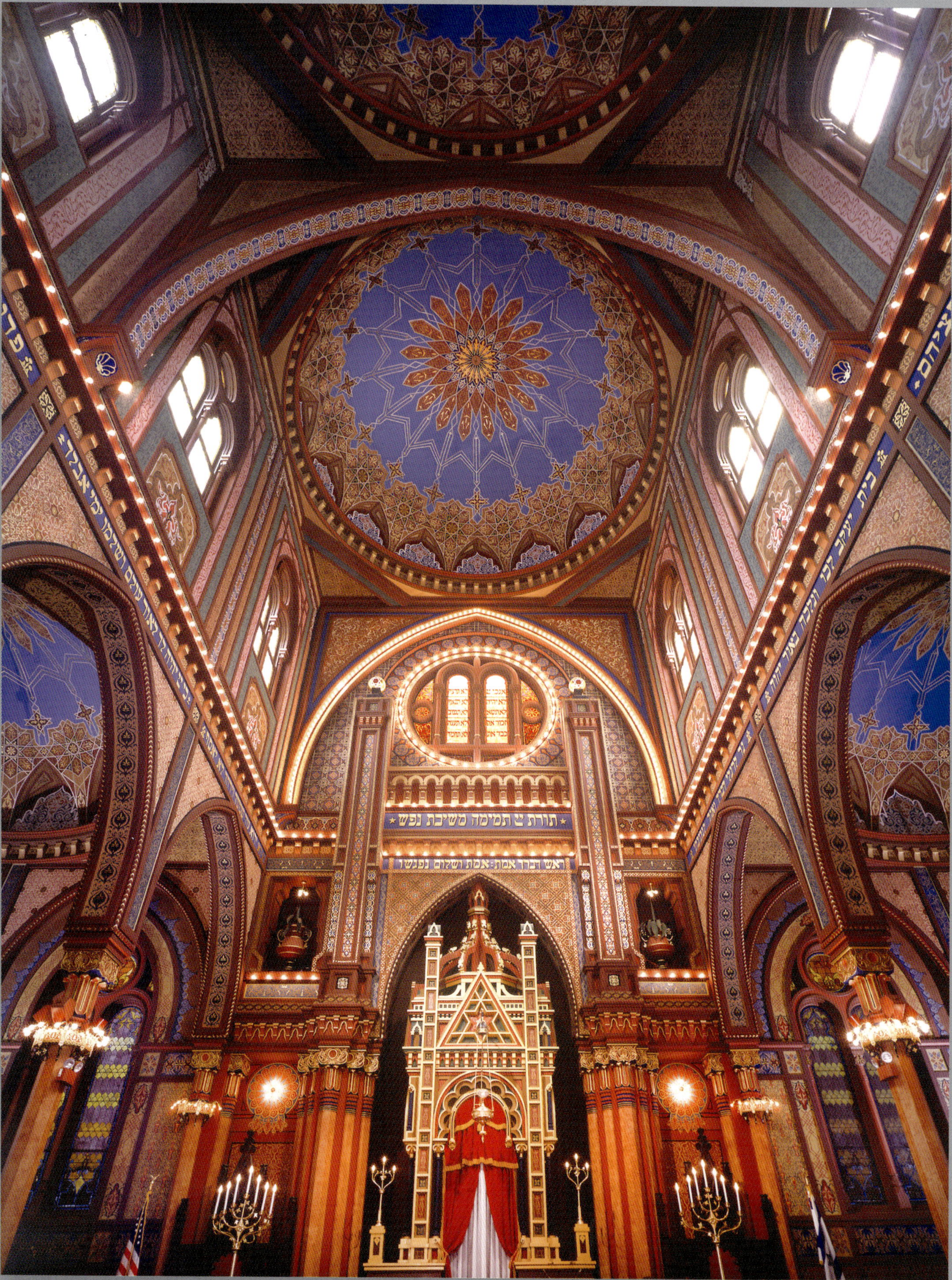
תורת יי תמימה משיבת נפש
ראש דברך אמת: אמת ושלום נפגשו

St. Peter in Chains Cathedral (above)

Consecrated in 1845, the neoclassical St. Peter in Chains Cathedral was the second permanent cathedral in the United States. It sits at the "Amen Corner" on Eighth and Plum streets, next to Cincinnati City Hall and facing Wise Temple. The soaring spire was the highest structure in the city when it was built.

St. Francis Xavier Church (opposite)

When the ornate Gothic Revival building was completed in 1861, it was the third church to occupy the site. Founded in 1819 by Jesuits, St. Francis Xavier was the first Catholic church in Cincinnati. Both St. Xavier High School and Xavier University had their beginnings in the building next door.

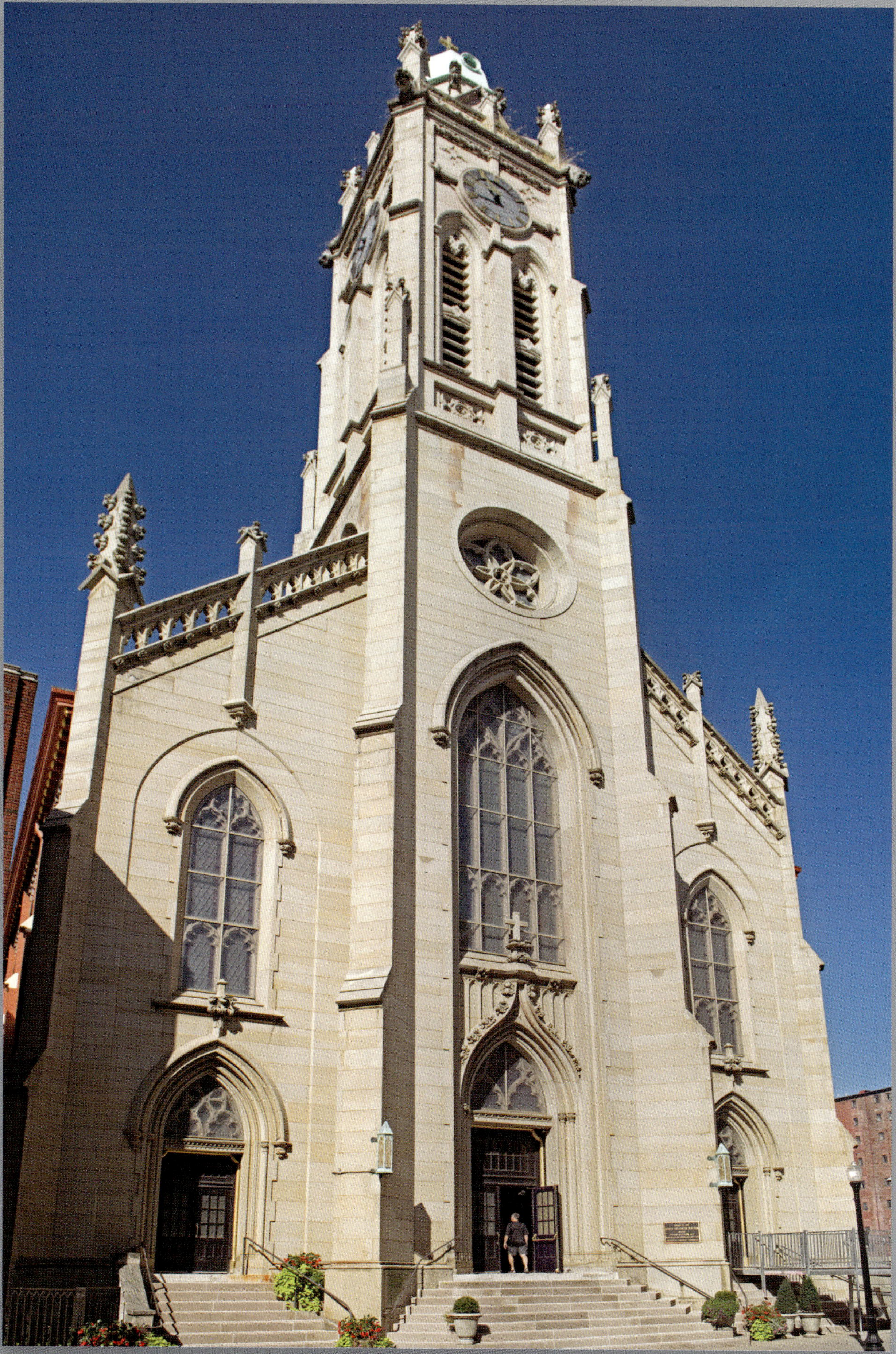

Smale Riverfront Park

Remember the giant keyboard in the movie *Big*? Cincinnati has one of its own: a "foot piano" tuned up and ready to play at Smale Riverfront Park. Built by the Verdin Bell Company using chimes salvaged from old churches, it's a stirring addition to the new park.

The Banks

City-county cooperation and public-private partnership are transforming the city's downtown riverfront. The Banks, a mixed-use development of restaurants, nightspots, offices, and chic residences, lies alongside spectacular Smale Riverfront Park. Together, they form a vibrant new neighborhood and a compelling destination for visitors of all ages.

Smale Riverfront Park *(top and bottom)*

Once flood-prone industrial land, the new Smale Park is a sweeping stretch of gardens, playgrounds, and outdoor recreation between Paul Brown Stadium to the west and Great American Ball Park to the east. The fruit-and-vegetable motif at the Castellini Esplanade (bottom) recalls the produce vendors who once worked here.

Carol Ann's Carousel *(above and right)*

For children, the highlight of a visit to Smale Riverfront Park is often a ride on Carol Ann's Carousel. The 44 figures on the custom-built carousel include animals designed with a local twist, such as an Ohio cardinal, a Bengal tiger, and a horse wearing a red baseball cap.

Anderson Pavilion *(pages 72-73)*

Lit up after dark, the carousel and its see-through glass house look like a jewel box at the center of the park. The complex was made possible by a private $5 million gift. It was created by an Ohio firm, Carousel Works of Mansfield.

ERSON PAVILION

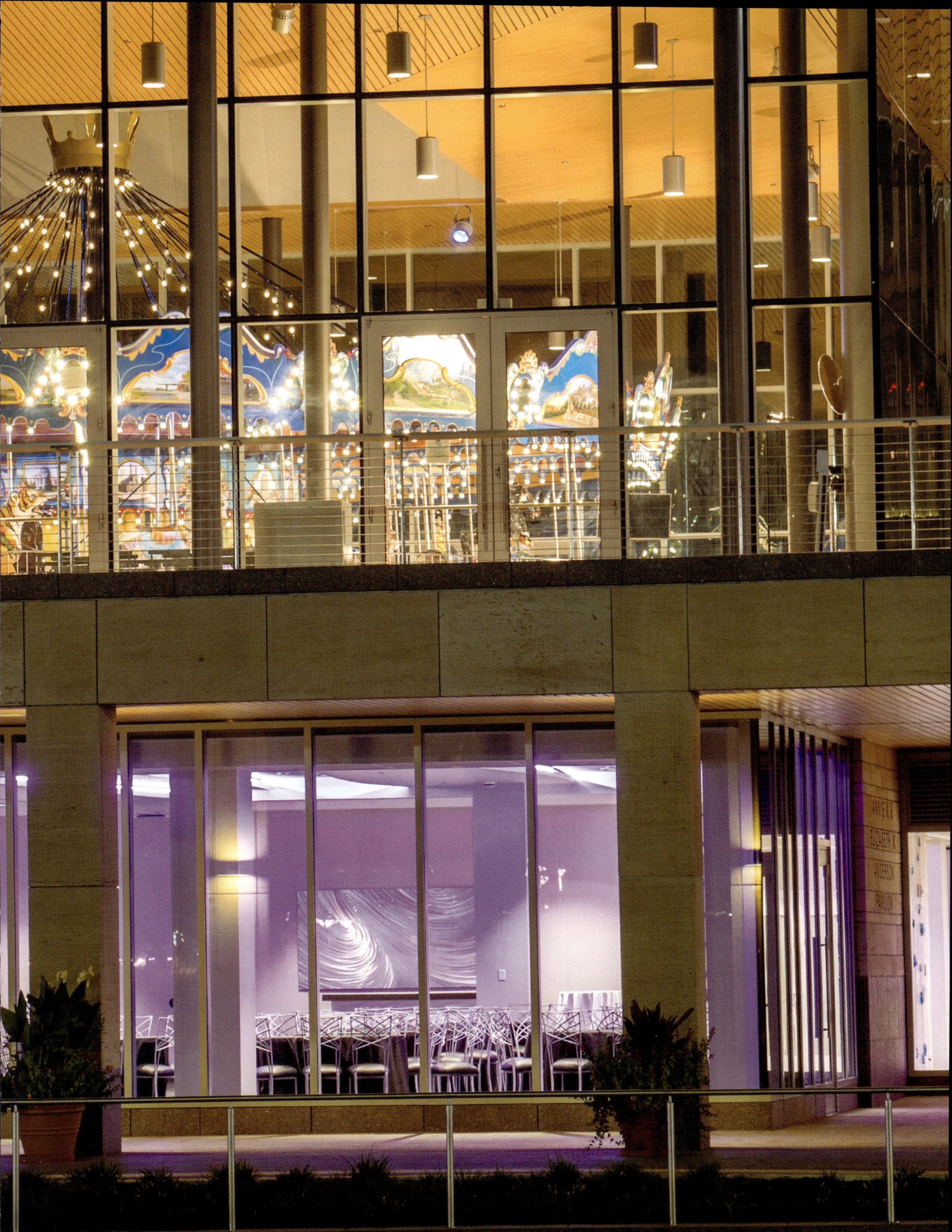

Smale Riverfront Park

The park lies on either side of the Roebling Suspension Bridge, and at night the illuminated bridge adds to the sparkling scene on a plaza sprayed by colorful water jets. Glass balconies offer a view of the park below and the river beyond.

Smale Riverfront Park Waterfall

The carousel complex is the centerpiece of a park that includes striking features such as this waterfall, where rainbow lights are illuminated in the evening. Water is a motif throughout the park, a reminder of the city's connection to the river.

75

Black Brigade Monument

In 1862, 718 African-American men volunteered to help build fortifications to shield the city from Confederate raiders. The monument in Smale Park recounts the history through plaques and statues such as this one by artist John Hebenstreit, in which Col. William Dickson receives a sword from Brigade Marshall P.H. Jones.

Black Brigade Monument

At the entrance to the monument, a table and chair symbolize the beginning of the story being told—in this case, a little-known tale of patriotism and dedication. The park designers, Sasaki Associates, worked with local artists to incorporate elements of the monument into the overall plan.

Black Brigade Monument *(above and left)*

Free black men were initially forcibly removed from their homes and taken off to work on Union Army fortifications. After a public outcry they were released; then hundreds offered their services of their own free will. The mother and child figures by sculptor Carolyn Manto recall the forced conscription.

Harriet Beecher Stowe House

Before she wrote the book that galvanized the abolition movement, Harriet Beecher lived here when her father, Rev. Lyman Beecher, headed Lane Seminary. Although she penned *Uncle Tom's Cabin* after moving back East, it is believed that her experiences here, hearing tales about escaping slaves, fueled her work.

National Underground Railroad Freedom Center

A "museum of conscience" that explores the global struggle for freedom, the National Underground Railroad Freedom Center tells the story of the route to freedom for enslaved people in the U.S. A log slave pen used by a Kentucky slave trader illustrates the dangers along the way.

National Underground Railroad Freedom Center

The building's curving architecture echoes the river's bends. Since its opening in 2004, the center has focused on those who have struggled to end slavery throughout history. It also engages visitors with speakers, conferences, and discussions about justice and human rights issues.

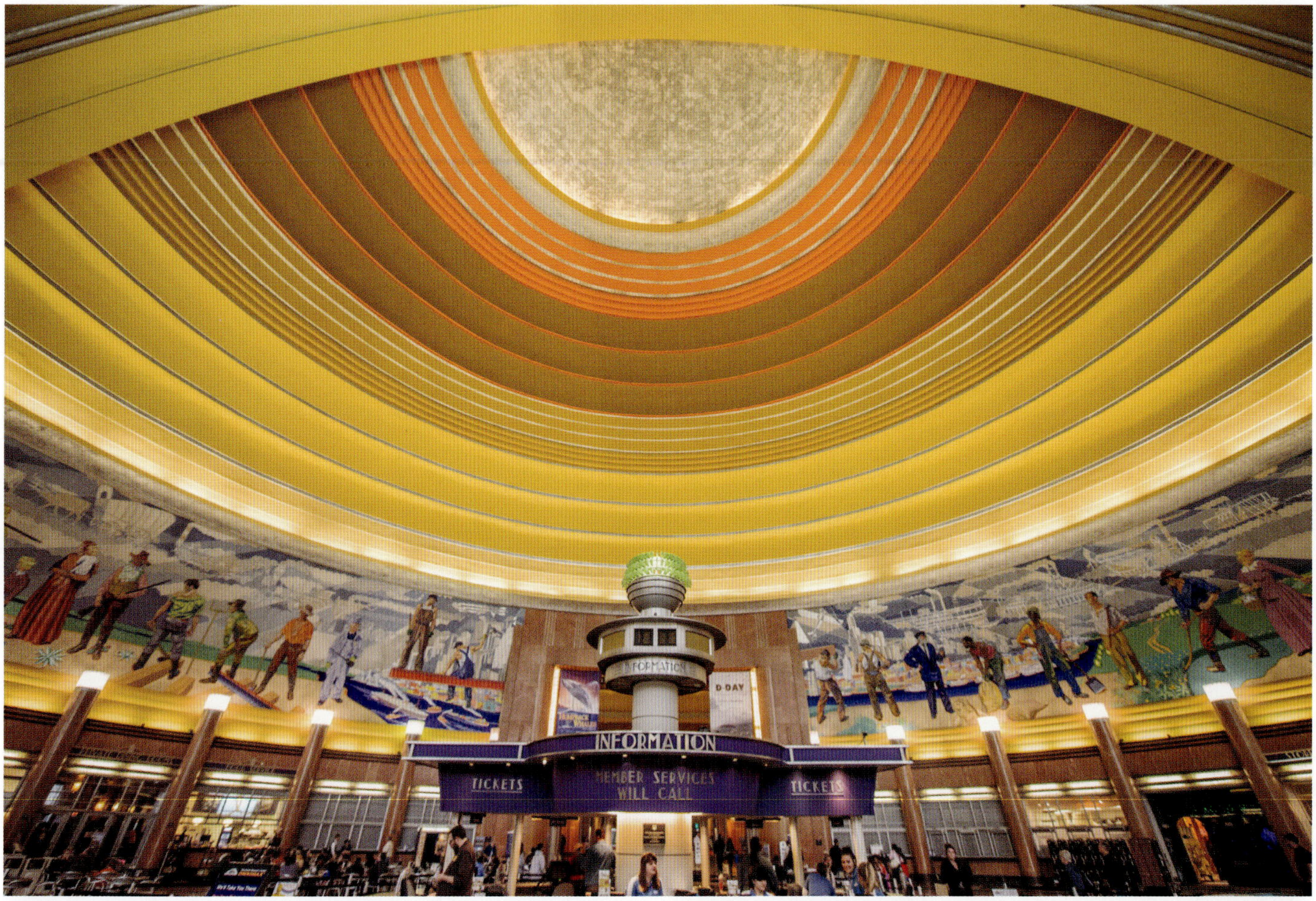
INFORMATION
TICKETS
WILL CALL
TICKETS
D DAY

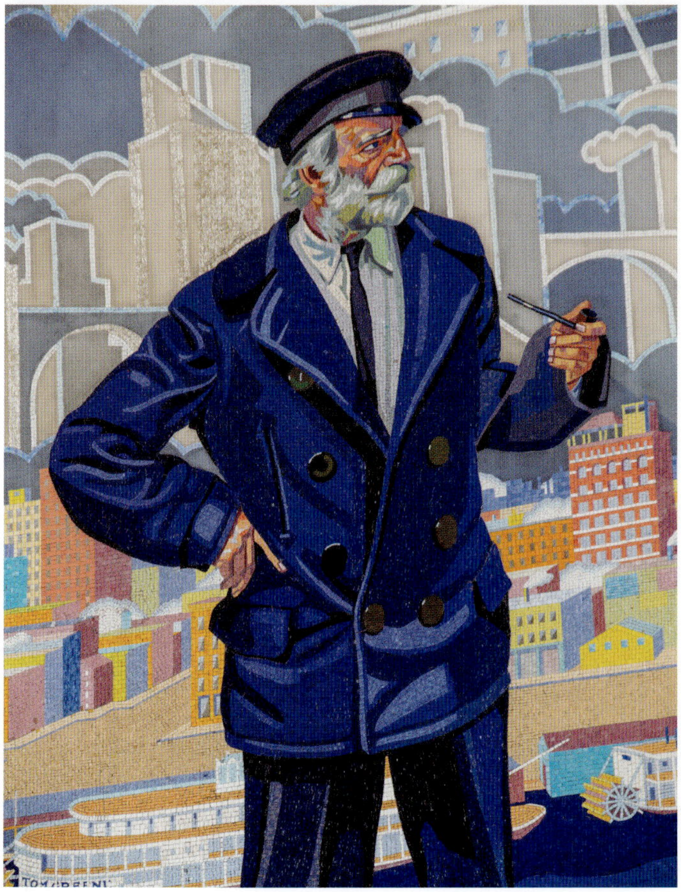

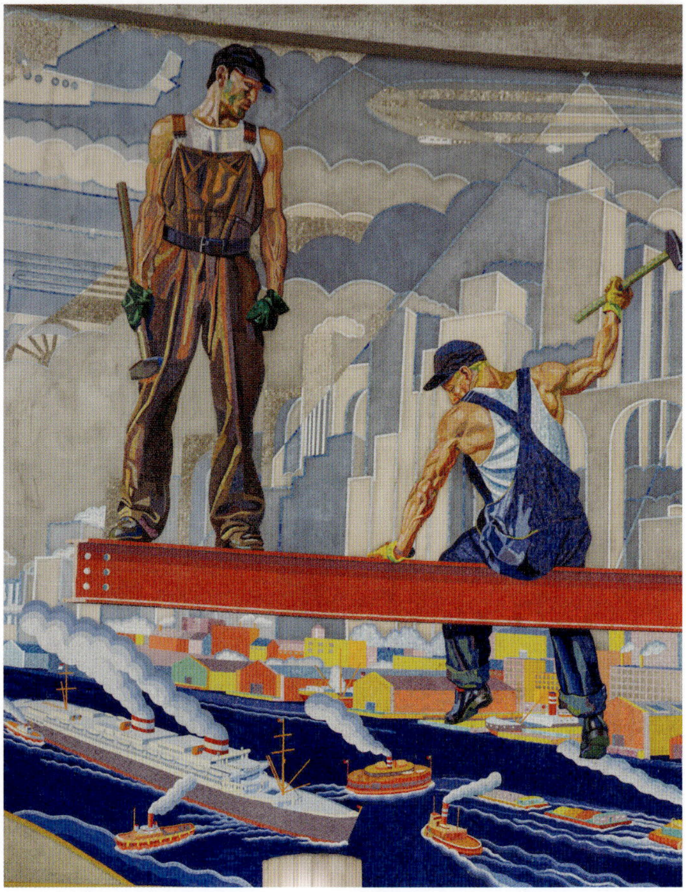

Union Terminal Murals *(opposite)*

Artist Winold Reiss created the vivid murals in Cincinnati Union Terminal of glass mosaic tile, so the figures are still vividly colored after more than 80 years. They surround a rotunda 106 feet tall and 180 feet wide. Only the Sydney Opera house has a larger half dome.

Cincinnati Museum Center

(above and pages 84-85)

The art deco masterpiece was dubbed "a temple to transportation" when it opened in 1933. It served a vital role in WWII; as many as 34,000 people a day made railroad connections here. Now called Cincinnati Museum Center at Union Terminal, it's home to multiple museums and an OMNIMAX theater.

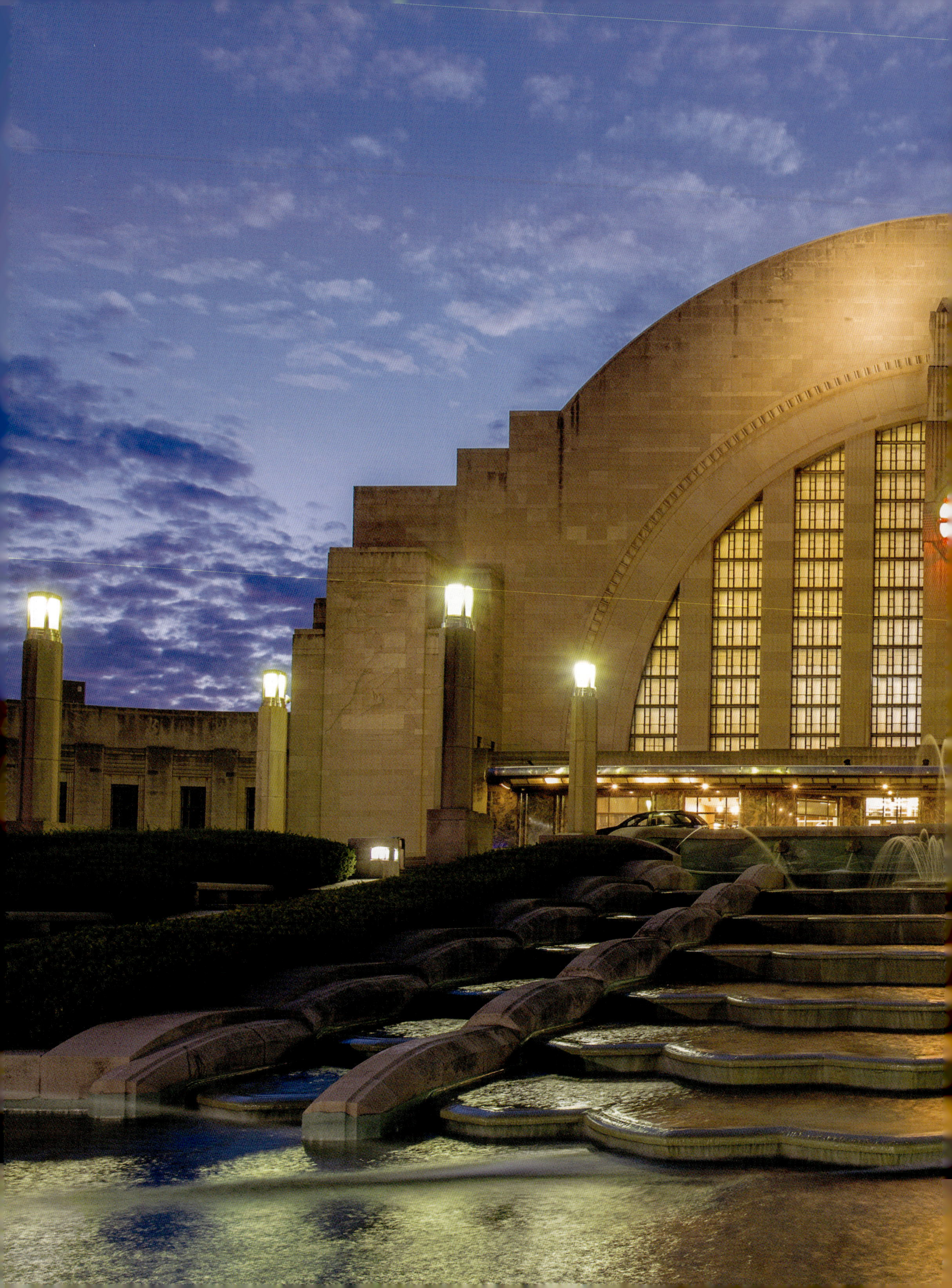

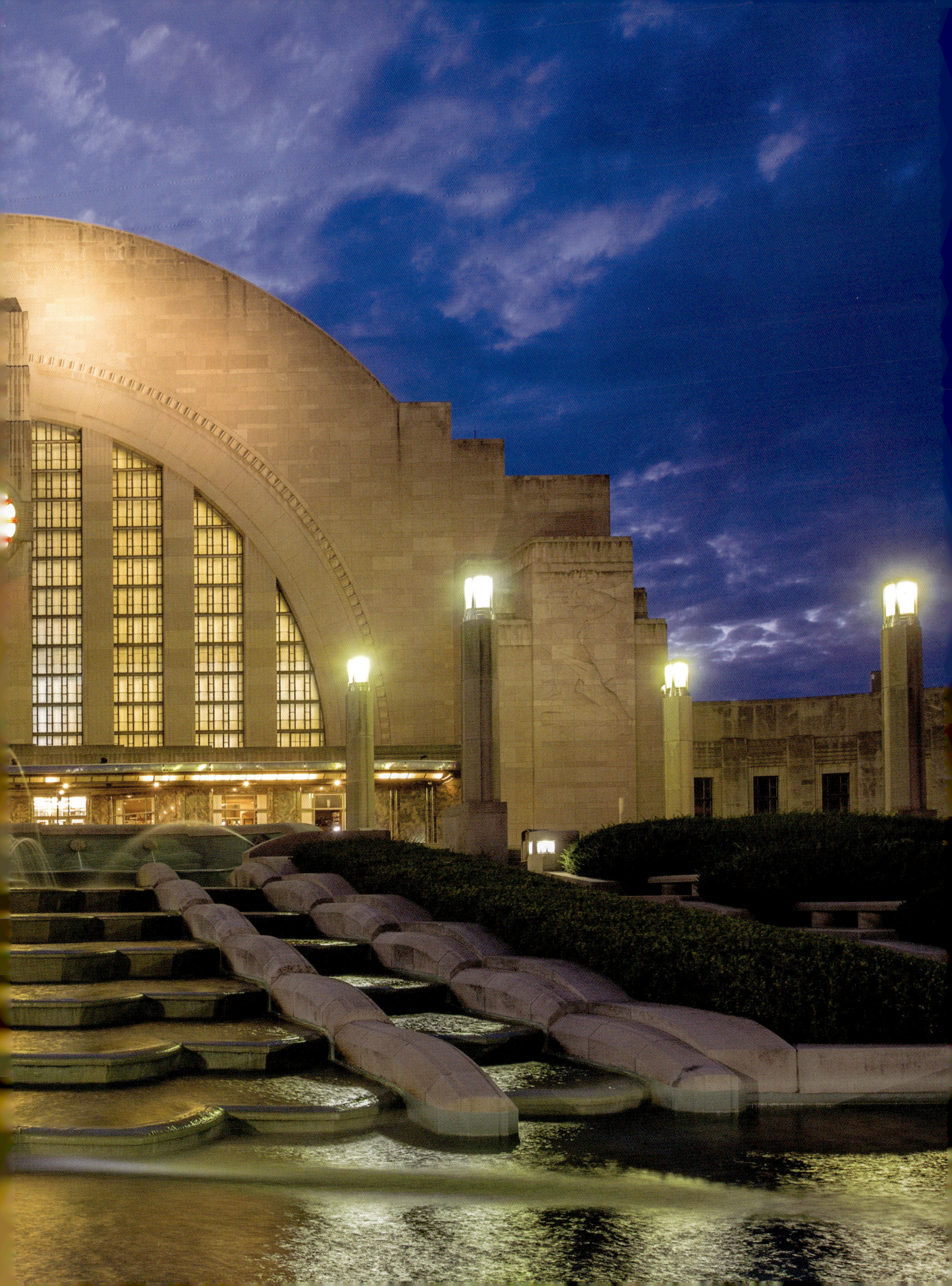

Cincinnati Zoo and Botanical Garden
(above and left)

The second oldest zoo in the U.S., Cincinnati Zoo has vintage structures such as the more than 140-year-old Reptile House. But its captive breeding program is state-of-the-art, and it supports field conservation efforts that use modern technology as well as traditional practices to protect and restore endangered species.

Cincinnati Zoo and Botanical Garden

(above and right)

One of the "greenest" zoos in the nation, Cincinnati Zoo's commitment to sustainability is everywhere. Pervious pavement and plantings keep storm water out of the sewers; there are low-flow toilets; zoo vehicles use biodiesel, and the Vine Street parking lot is covered with 6,400 solar panels to generate electricity.

Krohn Conservatory

During the annual spring butterfly show, thousands of butterflies flit through a themed garden specially created for the event. It's just one of the seasonal botanical shows, family events, and educational programs that draw thousands each year to the 1930's-era Krohn Conservatory in Eden Park.

Krohn Conservatory

The conservatory holds more than 3,500 plant species in four permanent rooms—the Palm, Desert, Tropical, and Orchid houses. At the center is the Palm House, with palms, rubber and banana trees, a goldfish stream, a 20-foot tall waterfall, and a romantic walk-through cave that runs behind the falls.

Krohn Conservatory *(above and left)*

In the late 19th century, Eden Park had greenhouses that were used for growing plants for the park itself. But eventually the value of a conservatory with public displays was apparent. Today, in addition to welcoming thousands of visitors a year, Krohn Conservatory is popular for private events, especially weddings.

Mt. Airy Forest

A wheelchair-accessible treehouse invites kids of all abilities to play. The nearly 1500-acre Mt. Airy Forest is home to an arboretum, picnic areas, and outstanding hiking and bridle trails. The heavily wooded park feels miles apart from the city that surrounds it.

Evening Skyline

Homeowners on the Ohio and Kentucky sides of the Ohio River like to debate who has the better view. Great American Ballpark ups the ante during night games, when Kentucky residents get the full effect of stadium lights and the fireworks that follow home runs.

Yeatman's Cove *(above)*

Cincinnatians love a party—especially on the riverfront. One of the most unusual has been the Tall Stacks Festival of Music, Arts, and Heritage. The event brought 17 replica and vintage riverboats from all over the country to Sawyer Point Park and Yeatman's Cove.

Serpentine Wall *(right and pages 94-95)*

The contoured steps of the Serpentine Wall are popular seating during events such as the annual end-of-summer Riverfest fireworks celebration. At quieter times, the steps are a favorite place to watch boats on the river. During spring flooding, the wall acts as a levee against the rising water.

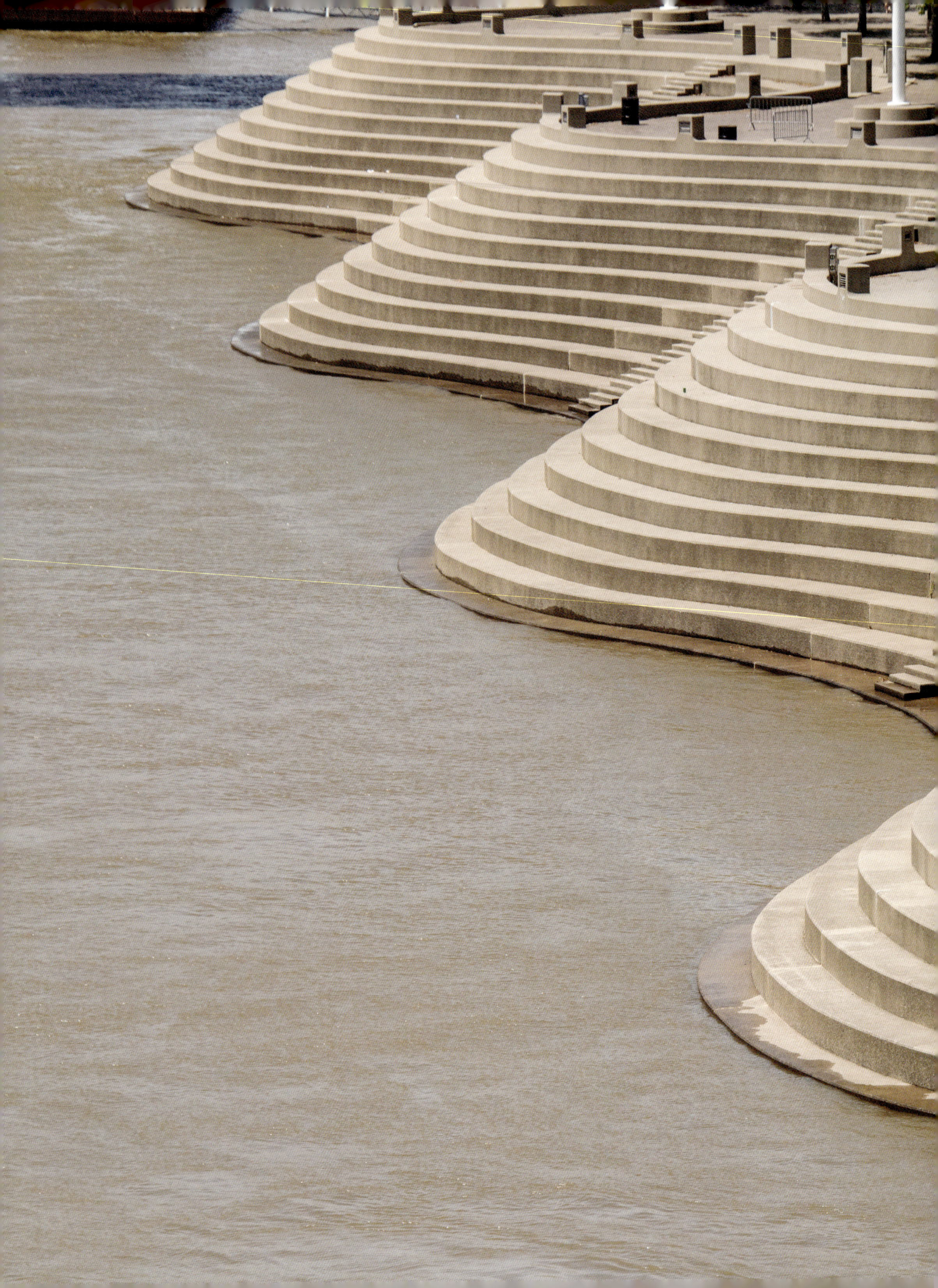

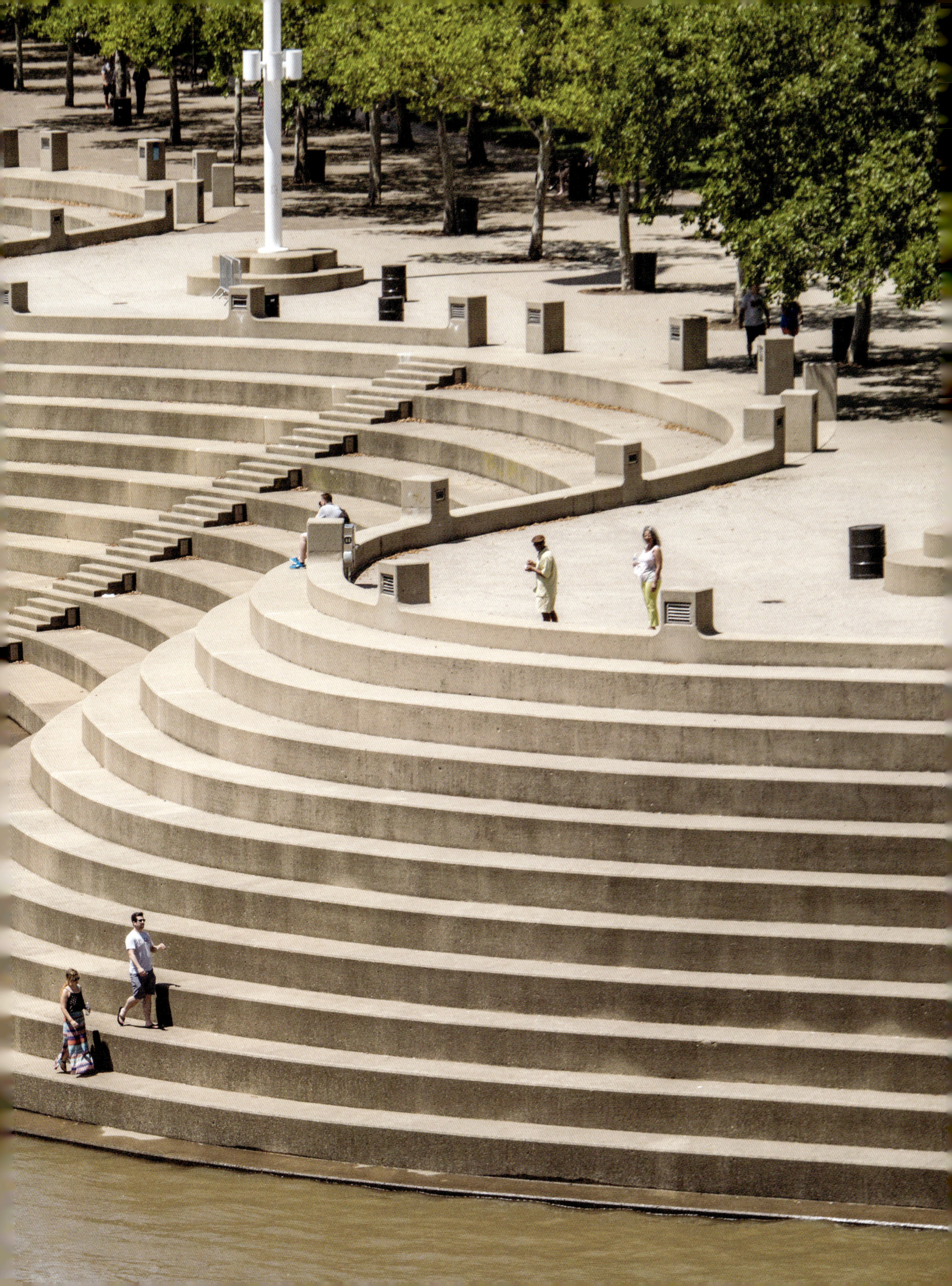

Bicentennial Commons (left and right)

Created for the city's 200th birthday in 1988, Bicentennial Commons at Sawyer Point mingles history with whimsy. The winged pigs designed by sculptor Andrew Leicester commemorate Cincinnati's 19th-century hog-packing industry. Initially somewhat controversial, today the "flying pig" is a Queen City icon.

Bicentennial Commons (opposite)

Symbols of the city's past are visible everywhere at Bicentennial Commons. Smokestacks recall the role of riverboats in the city's commercial life. A tall column marks the height of three devastating floods that ravaged the city. Most dramatic: the deadly 1937 flood, when water crested at 79.9 feet.

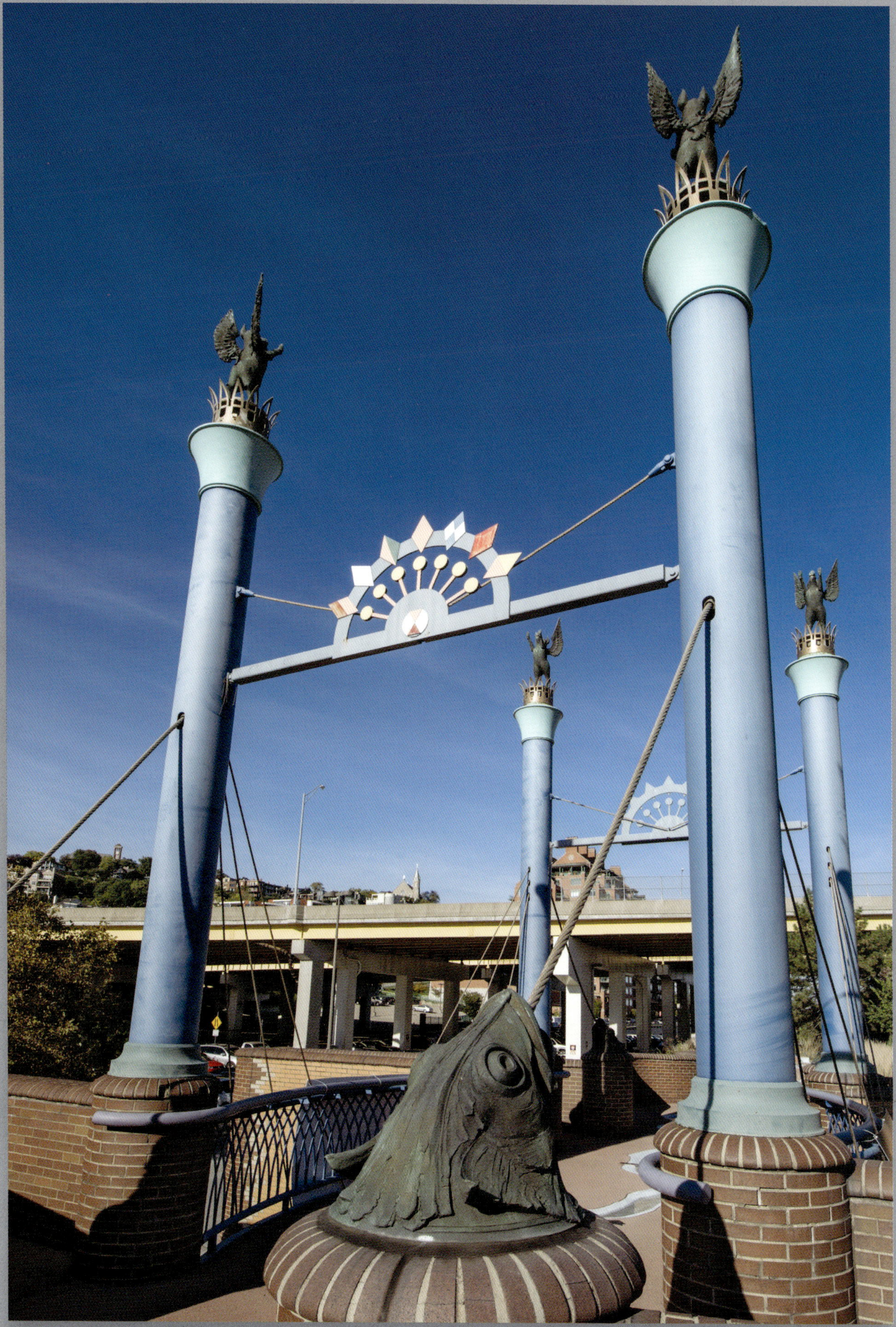

Sawyer Point

Outdoor concerts at the P&G Pavilion at Sawyer Point are a highlight of the summer in the city. Sawyer Point and Yeatman's Cove parks are also the site of Bunbury Music Festival. The annual three-day, multi-stage event draws upwards of 15,000 a day.

Cincinnatus Statue

The city was named after Roman war hero Lucius Quinctius Cincinnatus. In 458 BC, he was called from retirement to defeat barbarians threatening Rome. He did so quickly, then relinquished power and returned to farming. His statue in Sawyer Point depicts him turning back to life as an ordinary citizen.

Riverbend Music Center

The sweeping lawn of Riverbend Music Center is a magnet to music lovers of all sorts. Riverbend was built in 1984 as the summer home of Cincinnati Symphony Orchestra. Today, the busy schedule of pop, rock, and symphonic music draws people from across the region.

Riverbend Music Center

(top and bottom)

An aerial shot shows how Riverbend got its name. The colorful postmodernist venue, perched on the river east of the city, was designed by Michael Graves, a graduate of the University of Cincinnati. It has covered seating for 6,000 and space for many more in the fresh air.

101

Washington Park *(top and bottom)*

A $46 million renovation transformed historic Washington Park in the Over-the-Rhine neighborhood. The expanded park includes a stage, bandstand, dog park, civic lawn, a playground, and "spray ground" for children. The project was a partnership between the city, Cincinnati Parks Board, and Cincinnati City Center Development Corporation.

Cincinnati Music Hall *(opposite)*

Washington Park is bordered by one of the city's most beloved landmarks. Music Hall, the home of the Cincinnati Symphony Orchestra, Cincinnati Pops, Cincinnati Ballet, Cincinnati Opera, and the May Festival, and Springer Auditorium, the largest concert hall in the country.

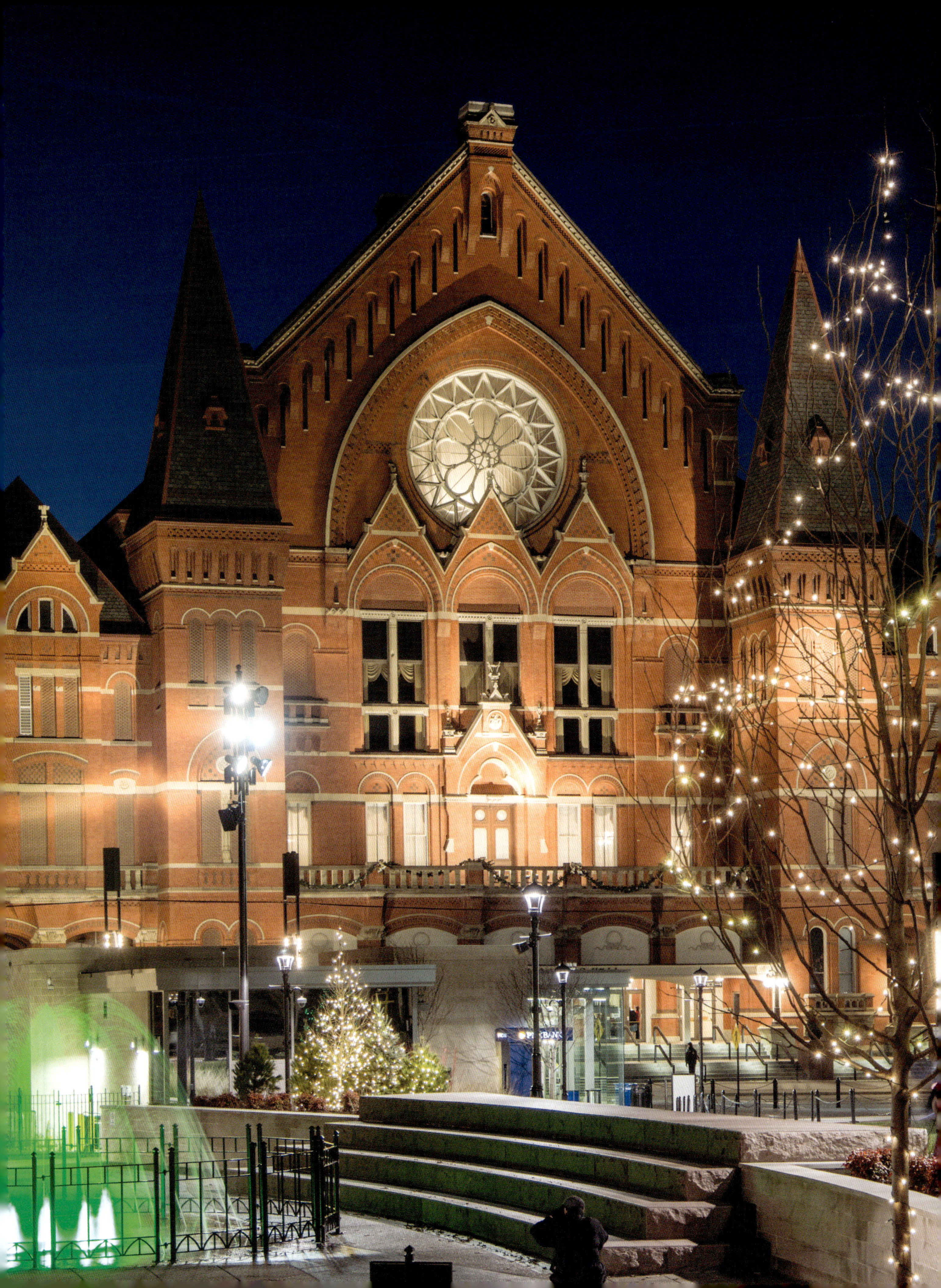

Labor Day Fireworks *(above and opposite)*

It began in 1977 as a party for a rock & roll radio station; now it's a tradition. Half a million people crowd the waterfront for the spectacular Western + Southern/WEBN Fireworks. Pyrotechnics exploding from barges and bridges are the work of Rozzi Famous Fireworks, a fifth generation Cincinnati company.

Lightning (pages 106–107)

Sometimes Mother Nature provides the show. This dramatic night view of the skyline captures a spring storm rolling in during a ballgame. On the left, the Roebling Suspension Bridge, PNC Tower, and Carew Tower are illuminated to show off their best features; to the right, the Great American Ballpark.

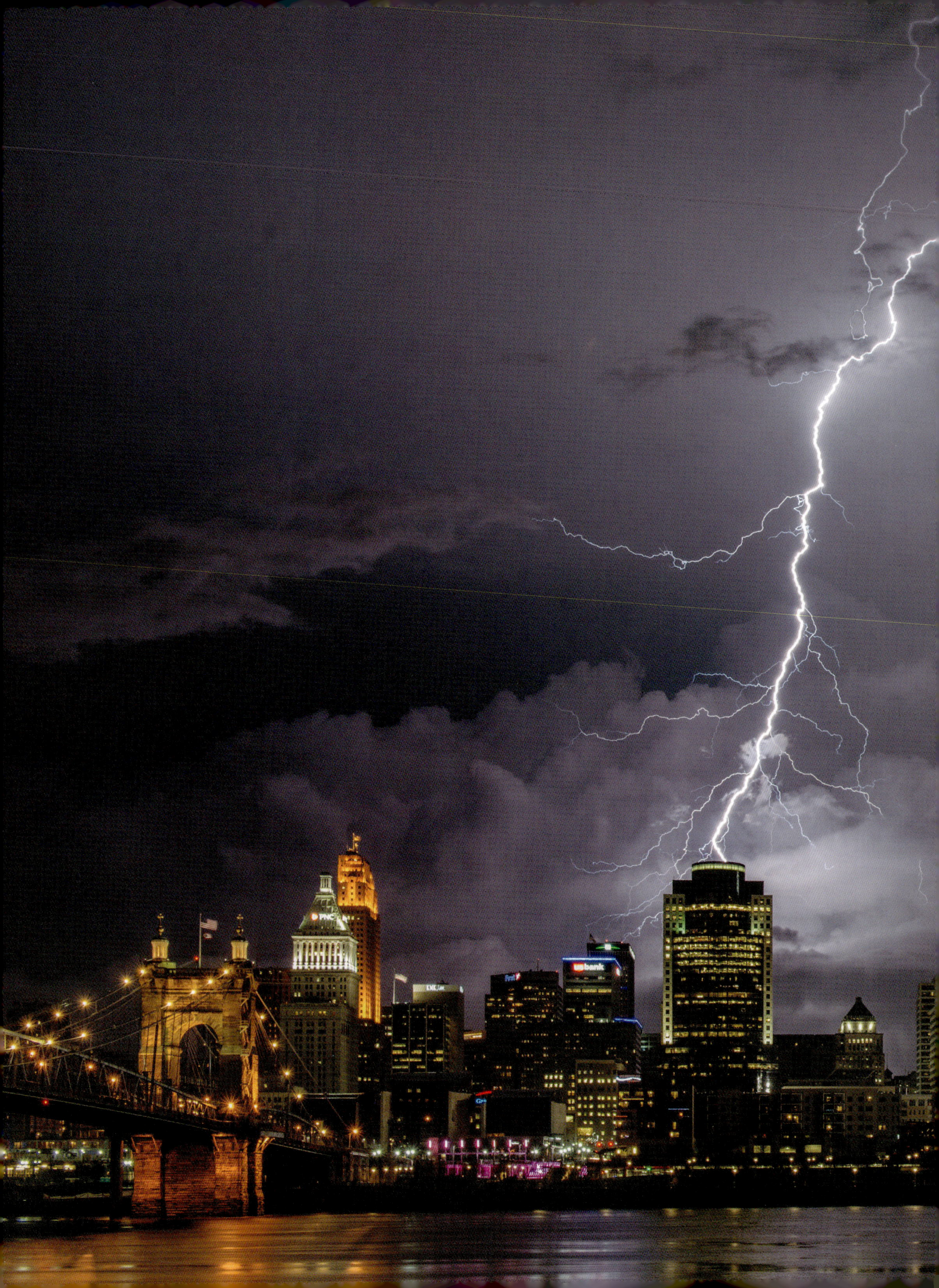
PNC

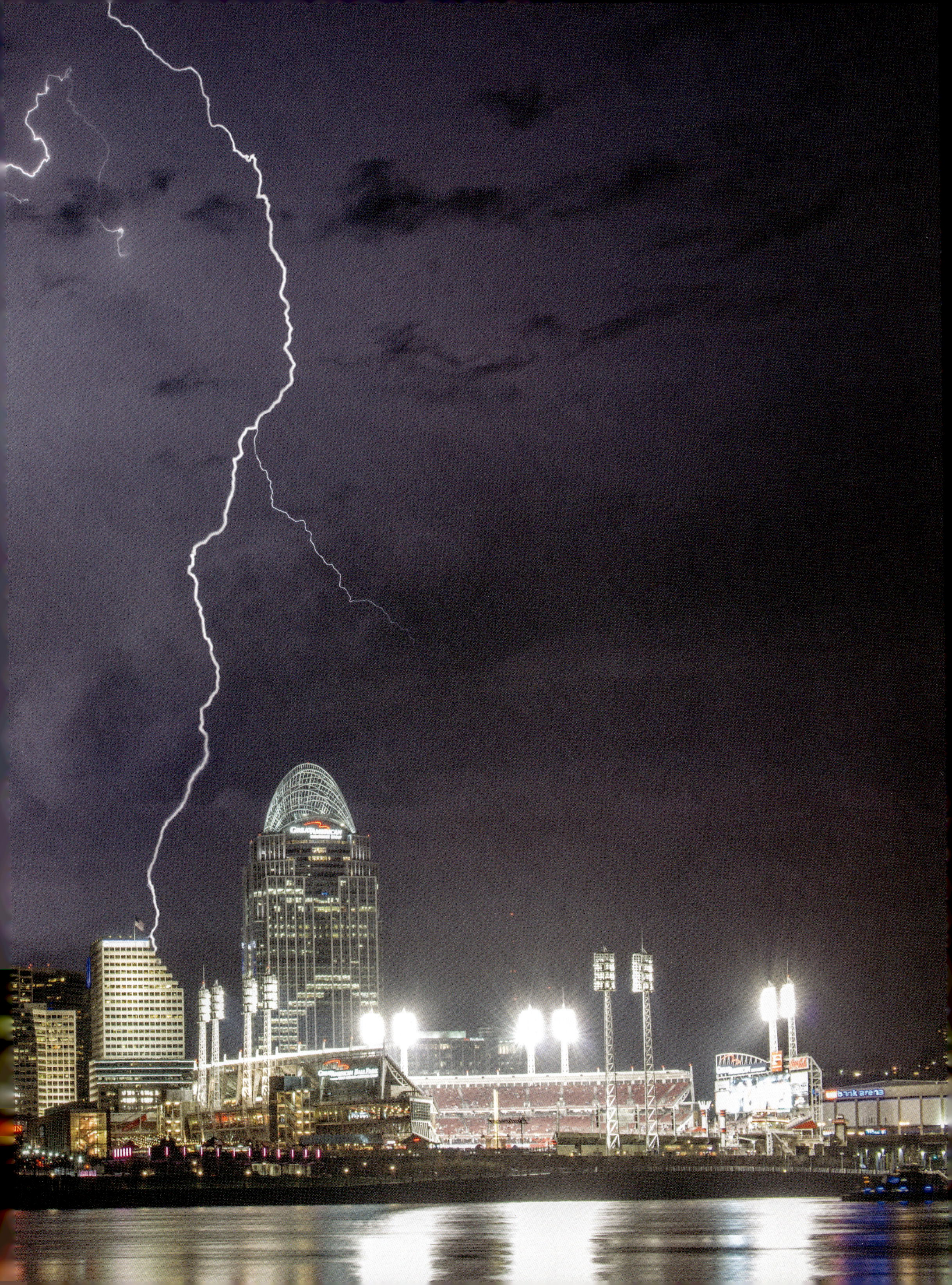
bank arena

Fireworks

Summer ends with a bang and the biggest fireworks display in the Midwest. Long before the excitement begins, crowds gather for Riverfest, a day-long, family-friendly, free (and alcohol-free) festival with entertainment at Sawyer Point and Yeatman's Cove.

Fireworks

Managing a crowd of 500,000—especially one that's spread along both sides of a river in two states—requires major coordination. Four bridges are closed; so are some streets. Even evening river traffic is shut down, and boaters aboard anchored vessels get a unique perspective on the sights and sounds.

Rubber Duck Regatta *(above and left)*

Yellow quackers—more than 150,000 of them—cascade from a truck into the Ohio during Riverfest. The annual ritual is a fundraiser for the Freestore Foodbank, a regional hunger program that supplies food pantries, homeless shelters, daycare centers, and senior service programs in 20 counties in Ohio, Kentucky, and Indiana.

Balloon Festival *(above and right)*

Mirror Lake in Eden Park is the setting for Balluminaria, a holiday event that brings hot air balloon enthusiasts to the park for a "glow" around the shallow reflecting pool. The walkway around the 3/4-acre pool is a favorite of joggers.

Aronoff Center for the Arts *(above)*

Designed by Argentinian-American architect Cesar Pelli, the Aronoff Center's striking façade, with its soaring lobby window wall, is the centerpiece of Walnut Street's lively entertainment district. The complex has an art gallery and three performance spaces, including the 2,700-seat Procter & Gamble Hall, where Broadway shows perform.

Contemporary Arts Center *(opposite)*

Half a block from the Aronoff, another landmark: the Lois & Richard Rosenthal Center for Contemporary Art. Designed by Iraqi-born British architect Zaha Hadid and completed in 2003, upon its opening, *The New York Times* declared it to be, "the best new building since the Cold War."

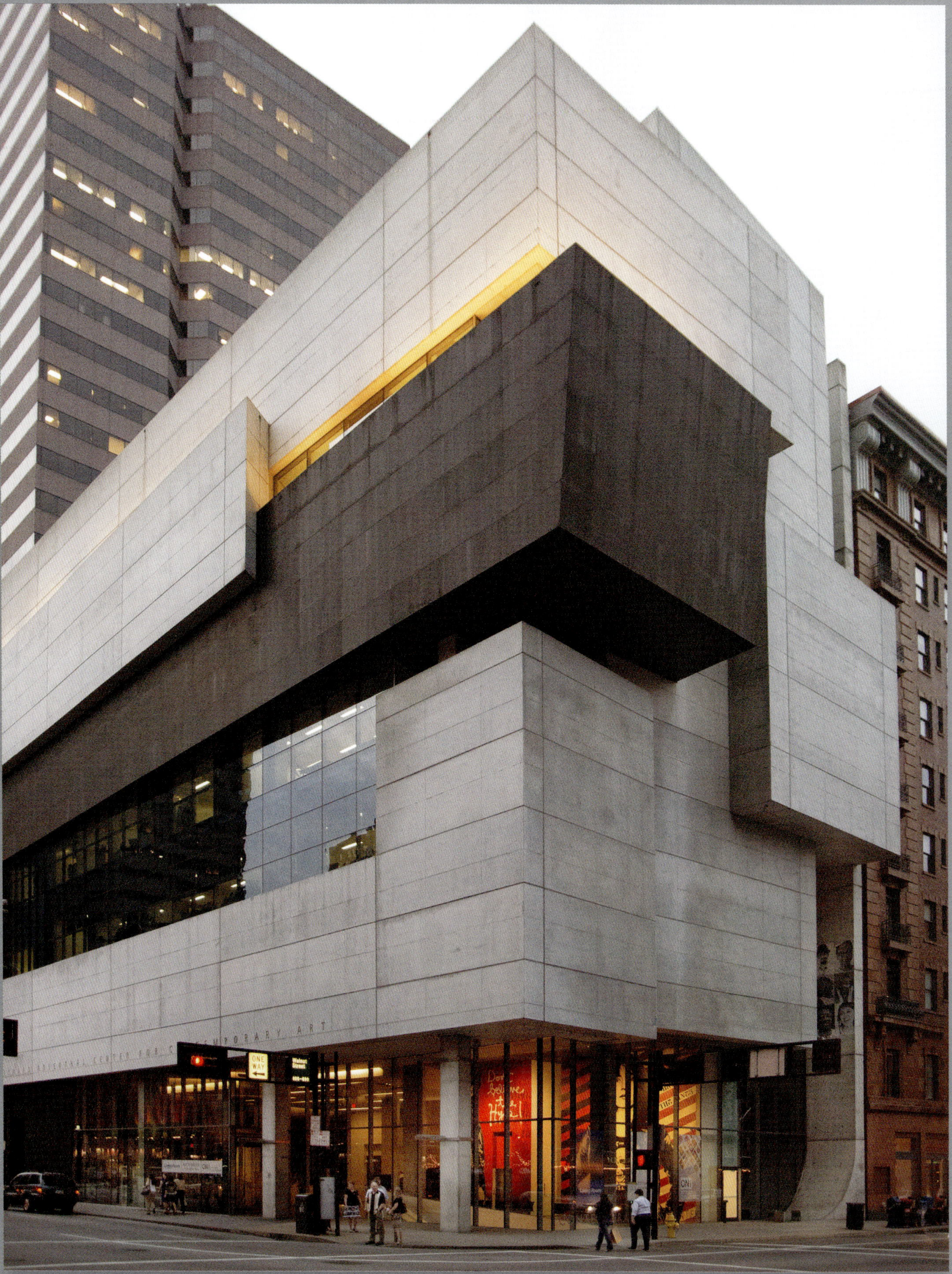
ONE WAY

Cincinnati Art Museum

Built in 1886 by wealthy citizens who donated their own collections, Cincinnati Art Museum is rooted in grand gestures. Thanks to a recent gift, admission to the 65,000-piece museum is admission-free forever. Outside, a gleeful Pinocchio sculpture welcomes visitors—the work of a native son, famed artist Jim Dine.

Duke Energy Children's Museum

Located inside the Museum Center at Union Terminal, the Children's Museum is packed with hands-on fun for kids of all ages, from The Woods—a climb-through forest—to a farmyard for toddlers. A partner in "Museums for All," the Children's Museum offers discounted admission to qualified families with financial need.

American Sign Museum

Do you remember MAIL POUCH TOBACCO painted on the side of a barn? Have your grandchildren ever seen Speedee, McDonald's original mascot? The placards, billboards, and flashing neon signs that tell the history of our country's changing times are showcased here.

American Sign Museum *(top and bottom)*
A fiberglass Big Boy welcomes visitors to the brightly-lit halls, and a recreated "Main Street" has storefronts displaying signs from different eras. And it's not all about nostalgia: there's a neon workshop with a window to allow visitors to watch modern "tube benders" at work.

117

Cincinnati Fire Museum *(above and left)*

This 1907 firehouse originally housed horse-drawn equipment. Today, it holds a museum filled with artifacts from the early days of firefighting, including an ancient steam pumper (below) and a huge drum used before the invention of mechanical alarms. Visitors can explore modern fire-fighting methods, too, and learn about home safety.

Firefighters Memorial *(opposite)*

The city of Cincinnati had a full-time, paid professional fire department as early as 1853. City officials, firefighters, and their families gather at the memorial on Central Avenue each October during Fire Prevention Week to commemorate lives lost in the line of duty.

CINCINNATI
FIRE DEPT.
IN HONOR OF THOSE DEDICATED FIREFIGHTERS
OF THE CINCINNATI FIRE DEPARTMENT
WHO LOST THEIR LIVES IN THE LINE OF DUTY
MAY 30, 1968
REDEDICATED OCTOBER 6, 2010

Police Memorial *(above and left)*

A small, quiet park opposite Cincinnati Police District One headquarters on Ezzard Charles Drive holds a memorial to the city's law enforcement men and women. The figure in the center is surrounded by granite markers that commemorate officers killed on the job.

Cincinnati Observatory

This 1873 observatory in the neighborhood of Mt. Lookout actually replaced one built in 1845 in Mt. Adams and dedicated by President John Adams. Today, it's a center for school groups and the public to learn about astronomy. The observatory boasts a working telescope used by eight generations of star-gazers.

Paul Brown Stadium (opposite top)

Built in 2000 and named after the founder of the Cincinnati Bengals organization, the Paul Brown Stadium quickly came to be known as "The Jungle." The 65,600-seat open-air facility with a distinctive cantilevered roof was designed to reduce end-zone seating and maximize sight lines.

Great American Ball Park
(above and opposite bottom)

In 2003, GABP replaced Riverfront Stadium/Cinergy Field as home to the Cincinnati Reds. But fans still can see the river, and the stadium's paddle-wheel and smokestacks are a reminder of the locale. The tall "toothbrush" light towers recall Crosley Field, the team's beloved home from the 1930s to 1970.

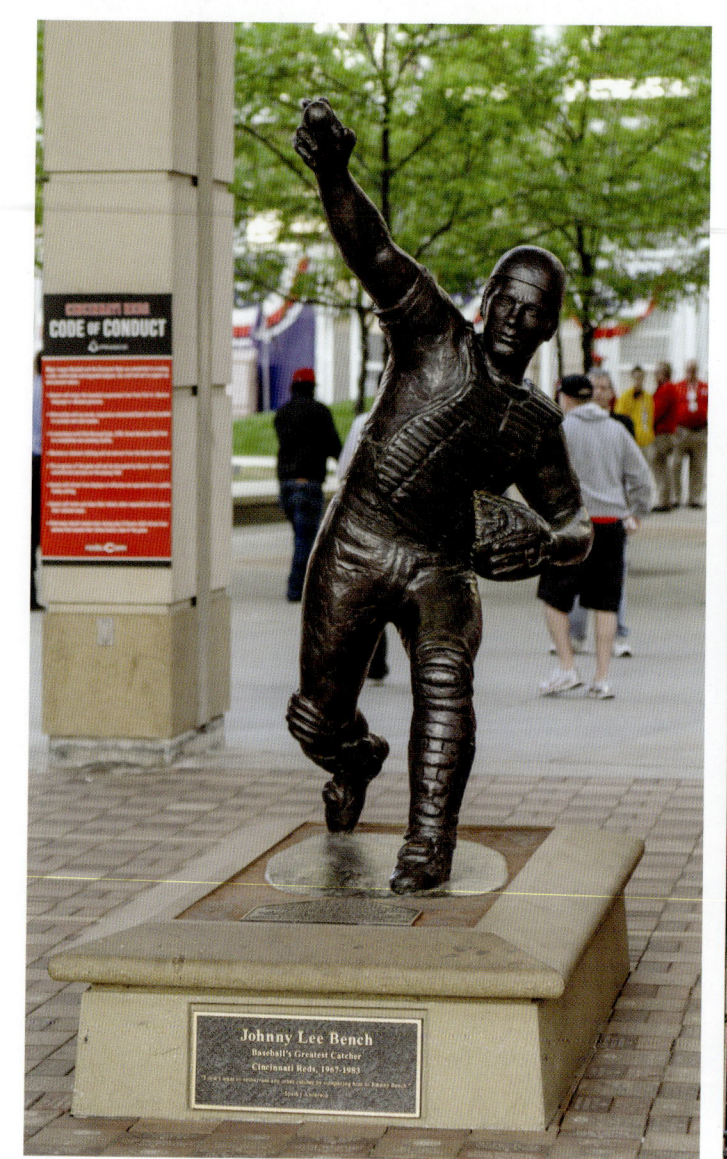

Johnny Bench Statue (left)

Baseball's greatest catcher is captured mid-throw in bronze on Crosley Terrace at the entrance to GABP. Commissioned by the Reds Hall of Fame, the Bench statue and other figures from the ball club's past were sculpted by Cincinnati artist Tom Tsuchiya.

Great American Ballpark (right)

The 50-foot-tall, limestone bas-relief mural looks as if it could be from the 1930s. Actually, it was created by 21st-century Ohio artist Mark Riedy. Called *The Spirit of Baseball*, it celebrates the city's long history with the sport.

Cincinnati Reds Hall of Fame and Museum (opposite)

The oldest team in professional baseball tells its story here. At the south end of the museum, a white rosebush in a sea of red blooms marks the spot where Pete Rose clobbered hit number 4,192 to beat Ty Cobb's record on September 11, 1985.

YOU TAUGHT ME TO AVOID THE TAG, TO SING THE KNOTTED HISTORY OF THE HIT KING WITH A STUBBORN TONGUE. TO SLIDE HEAD-FIRST INTO HOME.

Cincinnati Reds Hall of Fame (top)

The Big Red Machine is frozen amid displays highlighting the ball club's championship teams. Pete Rose, Ken Griffey, Joe Morgan, George Foster, Johnny Bench, Tony Perez, Dave Concepcion, and Cesar Geronimo—"The Great Eight"—are shown mid-celebration after the final play of the 1972 National League Championship Series.

Sparky Anderson (bottom)

Baseball uniforms through the ages tell the story of the evolving game and recall the unforgettable men who wore them. In the foreground, a bronze figure of Reds manager Sparky Anderson watches from a dugout display—a popular spot for visitors' photos.

World Series Display (opposite)

Inside the gift shop, a World Series display commemorates the team's greatest moments. But the museum has room for irreverent fun, too. There are kid-sized lockers, a broadcast booth where fans can try their hands at announcing, and the "ultimate Reds Room"--a recreated family den crammed with memorabilia.

127

Award-winning photography by **J. Miles Wolf** has become synonymous with the people, places, and events of Greater Cincinnati. For many, Miles' wonderful photographs of Downtown, Over-the-Rhine, the Ohio River, and other locations remain the impressions we remember, for he has a unique instinct for capturing the fabric and energy of Cincinnati. Miles is a prolific photographer who has cultivated multiple specialties in his 35-year career including landscapes, architecture, cityscapes, and sports. His work has appeared in national publications such as *Architectural Record*, *Better Homes and Gardens*, *National Geographic Books*, and *Popular Photography*. He currently uses high-resolution Nikon digital cameras for most of his work, but also shoots large format film on occasion. Thousands of his prints hang in private and corporate collections, and his photographs are part of the permanent collection of the Smithsonian's National Museum of American History as well as the Cincinnati Art Museum. *Cincinnati, Ohio: A Photographic Portrait* is his ninth book. In it, he captures the vibrancy of a city that treasures the past and builds for the future. To see more of his work, visit www.jmileswolf.com.

Linda Vaccariello visited Cincinnati for the first time in 1977. She went to a Reds' game, ate at a great restaurant, met some friendly people who took her to see the view from the Eden Park overlook, and concluded that this was a wonderful city. Three years later, in 1980, she moved here. And she discovered that she was right. Linda has spent her career writing about Cincinnati, its people, places, and institutions. With three decades on the staff of *Cincinnati Magazine*, she's had the opportunity to cover topics that range from architecture to zoo animals. Her work has been recognized by the City and Regional Magazine Association and the Ohio Excellence in Journalism Awards, among other honors. She lives with her husband in a townhouse that's in walking distance of City Hall, Washington Park, Union Terminal, the riverfront, and many of the other places captured in this book.